The Life and Times
of George Gipp

by

George Gekas

and books

south bend, indiana

THE LIFE AND TIMES OF GEORGE GIPP
Copyright © 1987 by George Gekas

and books, 702 South Michigan, South Bend, Indiana 46618

Library of Congress Catalog Number: 87-0000000
International Standard Book Number: 0-89708-164-1
    First Printing, 1987.
    Second Printing 1988.
    Printed in the United States of America
    3 5 7 9 10 8 6 4   Pbk.

Library of Congress Cataloging in Publication Data

Gekas, George.
The Life and Times of George Gipp.

Includes index
    1. Sports — United States — History —
    Miscellanea. I. Title.
[LB414.G11 1987] 351'.06'0164
ISBN 0-89708-164-1 Pbk.

Additional copies available:
> **the distributors**
> **702 South Michigan**
> **South Bend, IN 46618**

The Life and Times
of George Gipp

For
Helen and Marion

Foreword

by Paul Hornung

George Gipp was, perhaps, the greatest football hero who ever played for the University of Notre Dame. While much of his life was portrayed in the movie, *Knute Rockne-All American*, little is known of how Gipp actually was. Ronald Reagan's performance as the Gipper did not reveal the real Gipp, either on or off the field.

Gipp was a legitimate triple threat as a player. He could run, pass or kick. For years he held school records in all of these areas. This type of player has disappeared from the football field in recent years. Specialization has brought in players who can only do one or two things well. If you find a good running back, chances are he won't be able to block that well. Most punters can't kick field goals and most field goal kickers aren't able to punt. Gipp had the ability to do many things on the football field. He once drop-kicked a football 62 yards to win a game for Notre Dame. He averaged nearly 10 yards per carry during his junior and senior years.

The football achievements of George Gipp are quite remarkable. But, his exploits off the field are equally notable. What other great football legend was declared ineligible and expelled from school? What other player was able to gamble openly and place bets on his team while he participated in games? George Gipp was able to do these things.

I see much of myself in this biography, *The Life and Times of George Gipp.* I enjoyed being able to have some success at running, passing and kicking a football. In George Gipp, I see a player who was ahead of his time. His ability transcended the football field. This biography reveals some fascinating insights into Gipp as a man. It seeks to clarify the legend and paint an accurate picture of the great Gipper.

CONTENTS

Gipp's Finest Hour

November 13, 1920

The University of Notre Dame football team was set to play the University of Indiana Hoosiers. The Fighting Irish were prohibitive favorites. So much so that George Gipp had trouble finding anyone to bet on the Hoosiers.

The gamblers from South Bend could find few takers, even at odds of ten to one. The reluctance was understandable. Notre Dame was on its way to an undefeated, untied season. On the previous week Notre Dame smashed Purdue, 28–0. In that game George Gipp ran for 129 yards in ten carries and passed for another 128 yards.

Cecil Cooley, a guard for the Boilermakers remembered the frustrating afternoon. "Gipp was most evasive. He seemed to step sideways at the right time or hop over me. Many times I was sure I had him, but most of the time I ended up with empty hands. I can still remember looking around after he evaded me and see him going down the field weaving, sidestepping and twisting like a young colt that just got through an open gate."

George Gipp was only able to find one person willing to wager on Indiana. Gipp bet $10, but only after he agreed to wager that *he* would score more points than the Indiana team. Gipp had other problems before the Indiana game.

His girlfriend, Iris, was at the Claypool Hotel. After he dropped his sister off, he went up to see her. Iris told Gipp that she had married someone else. George later told a friend that he thought she had been making a fool of him.

Some 14,000 fans jammed into Washington Park to see what would be the toughest game Notre Dame had in years. For George Gipp, it turned out to be his roughest game. It was also the beginning of the end.

The Hoosiers were led by Charles 'Chick' Mathys, who ripped through the Irish front line through much of the first half. By the end of the third quarter, Indiana led 10–4. It looked like Notre Dame was about to blow its chance for an undefeated season and recognition as the top team in the country. George Gipp had been driven from the game after a rough tackle by two Hoosiers in the second quarter. By the beginning of the fourth quarter Gipp was on the bench with a separated shoulder.

Yet, somehow Notre Dame came back to make a game of it. Gipp's replacement, Johnny Mohardt, gained 25 yards on one play and 18 yards around left end on another. The ground game was suddenly back in form. Mohardt and Norman Barry, running on alternate plays smashed their way to the Indiana one-yard line. But, two plays up the middle gained nothing.

It was now third down and Gipp was sent back into the game. The Indiana line knew that Gipp would get the ball and braced itself. Gipp was stopped cold. On fourth down, Gipp got the ball again and battered his way into the end zone. He ran into the goal posts and almost sent it tumbling to the ground. Gipp converted the point after and Notre Dame trailed by three.

Time was running out as Gipp kicked off. He was in on the tackle and left the game again after hurting his left shoulder. The defense then stiffened. Indiana lost five yards on the next two plays, and on third down Eddie Anderson broke through the line and caused the Indiana back to fumble.

Mohardt and Barry then moved the ball to the Hoosier 15 yard line. Mohardt was shaken up and Gipp re-entered the game. Gipp took the snap, and instead of drop-kicking for the three points that would tie the game, passed to Anderson at the one yard line. On the next play, while the Indiana line braced for Gipp, Joe Brandy kept the ball and went in for the score. Gipp missed the conversion, but, with time running out, it didn't really matter. Notre Dame had won, 13–10, and had preserved its undefeated season.

Mathys, who went on to become a big star in the NFL, called the game the most frustrating of his entire career. "It is the one game in my football career of so long ago that I have replayed over and over again in my memory, but it still comes out to a defeat. We led the national champions in every department, but a costly fumble — our only fumble — lost it for us."

Indiana had a chance to tie the game in the closing minutes of play, but, a field goal attempt was just wide off the mark.

Eugene Kessler, a reporter who covered the game for *The South Bend Tribune*, called it "the greatest comeback ever recorded" but called much of the effort poor. "They had their off day, and to spectators who never saw them play, they looked very poor and offered crumbly defense."

For Gipp, it was a painful afternoon. Indiana had clearly made him a marked man. His shoulder was in such bad shape that it affected his passing and greatly hindered his running. After the game Gipp had dinner at the Claypool Hotel with Coach Rockne. Mathys later joined them and they had a long, friendly talk. Later in the evening Gipp went to the Lincoln Hotel and ran into John Welch. Earlier in the day Gipp had given Welch $100 to bet on Notre Dame, but the bookie was only able to place $65 of the bet while giving the Hoosiers 15 points. Welch gave Gipp the money he couldn't place. Gipp hugged him and said, "John, thanks. It's the first time I've smiled today."

The Notre Dame team left Indianapolis and boarded a train for South Bend. Two games remained on the schedule, Northwestern and the Michigan Aggies (later to become Michigan State). However, as the train headed back to the campus, there was word that a game with Penn State, the undefeated powerhouse team from the East, was being arranged for December 4th. It would be a dream matchup, which would decide once and for all, the national championship.

While the rest of the team got off the train in South Bend, George Gipp stayed on and went to Chicago. He had promised that he would help a former teammate, Grover Malone, the coach at Loyola Academy, teach his team the art of drop-kicking.

So, on a cold blustery day, Gipp gave a football clinic. An icy wind blew across the field as Gipp spent at least three hours demonstrating the intricacies of the drop-kick. After the clinic, Gipp returned to South Bend. On the train he began to feel a cold coming on. After he returned, he confined himself to bed. He was still sick when Coach Rockne saw him on the day before the Northwestern game.

"Think you're up for the trip?" Rockne asked.

"I suppose so," Gipp replied.

"If you're not feeling up to par when we get there, I don't intend on using you," Rockne said.

"That's jake with me."

But, once Gipp got on the train for Evanston, there was little chance that he wouldn't see action in the Northwestern game.

The Northwestern game was a big one for the Notre Dame Alumni Association, especially for fans and alumni who lived in the Chicago area. Notre Dame had not played a game against Northwestern since 1903. For many, it would be the only chance they would have to see Gipp play.

Practically the entire campus was making plans to journey to Evanston for the game. At 8 a.m. a special South Shore train left South Bend for Chicago, where a special Chicago Elevated Co. train was set to make a run to Evanston.

Rockne had indicated that he wanted to keep Gipp out of the game. In addition to his shoulder injury, Gipp was suffering from a slight cold. The prudent course would be to rest him. For a few days before the game, a specialist was treating Gipp and attending to his injuries. Despite the injuries, it would still be a great disappointment if Gipp were not able to play in front of Notre Dame's Chicago alumni. On game day, the largest crowd in years packed the Northwestern stands, more than 20,000.

By today's standards, a crowd of 20,000 for a football game would not be extraordinary. Often crowds of well over 100,000 attend college games at the University of Michigan. But, as it turned out, the Northwestern game had more fans than any game that Gipp ever played in. By the end of the 1920s, Notre Dame regularly played before crowds of 50–60 thousand. This is a tribute to Coach Rockne, the Notre Dame football team and the increased popularity of the sport.

When the Northwestern game began, George Gipp was on the sidelines. Many fans did not know that Gipp was sick, and throughout the game they chanted incessantly, "We want Gipp! We want Gipp!"

After struggling through the first quarter Notre Dame built a comfortable lead. By the time the fourth quarter rolled around the game was no longer in doubt. But, the crowd was getting impatient. Rockne could ignore it no longer. He sent Gipp back into the game. Despite a high fever and a bone-chilling wind coming off Lake Michigan, Gipp entered the fray.

The team changed its tactics with Gipp in the line-up. The score dictated running plays but Gipp's condition made passing the ball and avoiding contact wiser. So, instead of lining up behind the center, Gipp dropped back into a "shot-gun" formation and passed the ball. It was a remarkable display, as he completed 5 of 6 passes for 157 yards.

"Rockne told him to pass, but not to run," said Norman Barry, a teammate. "So, we lined up in punt formation to give him better protection. The ball was snapped to Gipp, and he threw a pass that traveled 55 yards into the air. I caught it and ran for the touchdown." The 70-yard pass play was the longest in Notre Dame history up until that time. The record stood for several years.

Toward the end of the game, Gipp fielded a Northwestern punt. Two Northwestern players approached him and guided him down gently. It was a display of sportsmanship that befitted a great athlete in his final game. Notre Dame won the game 33–7.

After he returned to South Bend, Gipp's cold got worse. His body temperature had become very high. Later, Gipp told Rockne that he was feeling terrible. Rockne made all the arrangements and Gipp entered the hospital.

Three weeks later George Gipp died.

Beginnings

The northern part of Michigan's upper peninsula is an elongated piece of land that begins at the mainland and ends 56 miles later at Lake Superior, the largest body of fresh water in the world. The area is extremely vulnerable to winter winds. It is commonly called the Keweenaw Peninsula. This is where Gipp was born and where he grew up.

It is a notable area in U.S. history. The peninsula was the scene of the first mining boom in North America, but it wasn't gold that made the area thrive, for it contained the richest deposits of copper in the world. Six years before the 1848 Gold Rush at Sutter's Mill in California, thousands of people came to Keweenaw to mine copper. At least 31 different nationalities representing people from all over the world came to Keweenaw during the copper boom.

George Gipp's paternal ancestors were German. His grandfather, Antoine Gipp, was born in Lutzrath, Prussia in 1820 and came to the United States to escape political persecution following a failed revolution in 1848. Newspaper stories carried reports of the copper find and Antoine Gipp was determined to go to reports of the copper find and Antoine Gipp was determined to go to Michigan to get into mining. He spent four years getting money together and eventually moved to Michigan in 1857. The Gipp family finally settled on a long tract of land that was property of a local mining company, in an area that was to become the village of Laurium. It was there that the last of the Gipp children were born: Lizzie, Kate and Louis.

During those years Antoine Gipp was a laborer for the Calumet & Hecle Consolidated Mining Company. The copper boom, however, proved to be illusory. For many people it was more of a bust. Many of the fortune hunters who rushed to Michigan found that while there was copper, getting it out of the ground proved to be difficult. For six years Antoine Gipp struggled on, as copper production had tapered off.

The copper had been discovered in 1853 by Ed Hulbert, who found the first mineral deposits, but did not have the needed money to develop a full-scale mining operation. He went to Boston were he received financial support from Quincy Adams Shaw, the head of a prominent family.

On September 17, 1864, a great copper lode was discovered which was headlined in newspapers throughought the east. Hulbert and his partners founded the Calumet Mining Company. Nearby, however, another tract of land was suspected to contain most of the copper ore in the area and another company, The Hecle Mining Company, was formed to purchase this new site for $60,000 from St. Mary's told of how Hulbert had a personal failure when he began his mining operation.

When Quincy Shaw and his fellow investors added up the cost sheets, they found that Hulbert was spending a great deal of money with little copper to show for it. It was true that Ed (Hulbert) had succeeded in accumulating large quantities of the rich conglomerate rock in stock piles, but he was getting nowhere mining and smelting it. Rich as the red pudding stone might be, obviously it would bring no cash into the company treasury until it was converted into copper ingot. Yet, all the while Hulbert contradicted the bleak figures of the cost sheets with optimistic letters to Quincy Shaw.

Shaw sent his brother-in-law, Alexander Agassiz, to inspect the mine. Agassiz had previously cleaned up a messy operation for Shaw in Pennsylvania. When he came to the peninsula he found that Hulbert was running a terribly inefficient operation. After a confrontation with Hulbert, Agassiz was finally put in charge of the mine.

In 1862, Antoine Gipp enlisted in the Union Army. He was 42 when he enlisted and later saw action in the Battle of Gettysburg. During a battle at Spotsylvania, Virginia, Gipp was severely wounded in the right arm. On July 26, 1865, he was discharged, just five days after being promoted to the rank of sergeant.

His service in the Army imposed some great hardships on his family which was forced to break up until the war was over. Matthew Gipp, who was born in 1854, and was the second of Antoine and Agnes Gipp's children, was temporarily adopted by a family who lived in the nearby village of Eagle River.

His service in the Army imposed some great hardships on his family which was forced to break up until the war was over. Matthew Gipp, who was born in 1854, and was the second of Antoine and Agnes Gipp's children, was temporarily adopted by a family who lived in the nearby village of Eagle River.

Following the Civil War, the Calumet and Hecle Mining Company became more and more successful. Under Agassiz's leadership, stock in the company reached record heights. The company became the predominant industry in the area. It owned nearly all the land and managed all the property. It was a boom town. Houses were built and rented to miners for between six and eight dollars a month. C&H Mining Company was the first major company in North America to provide a company hospital and the first to provide an employee benefit fund to cover sickness and death. Wages for workers in the mine and related industries were well above the national scale.

Matthew went on the C&H payroll as a carpenter. On June 16, 1877 he married Isabella Taylor, whose parents escaped the Irish potato famine in the 1840s and settled in Massachusetts before coming to Michigan.

The Gipps gave birth to eight children, with George being the seventh. George Gipp was born on February 18, 1895 and lived at 432 Hecle Street, in a house built by his father. The other children included: Alexander, Matthew, John, Louise, Mary, Bertha and Dorothy. His baby sister, system in the area was, by most accounts, excellent. The teachers were the highest paid in the country, helped greatly by the benevolence of C&H. When he was twelve, Gipp transferred to John Duncan School, where he would be until he transferred to a junior high school in Calumet.

George Gipp's record in school, by all accounts, was poor. He hardly ever did homework, and seemed to delight in not conforming to school discipline, making jokes and upsetting the classroom. Frederic Larson, a classmate at Calumet High School, who went on to Notre Dame, said George was frustrated as a student.

"He reminded me of a young stallion that would rear up, pull back, and then go forward, moving from side to side, all because it disliked anything that looked like it would restrict its freedom." George hated to be restricted. He also could be exceedingly witty and always had a ready response for any situation. He had difficulty staying in school long enough to compete in sports because the authorities often expelled him for some prank or sharp remark he would make to a teacher. Once I felt the brunt of a Gipp remark myself. It was in our geometry class at Calumet High. I do not recall the question asked me by our teacher; I only recall answering that the figure in question was an isosceles triangle. Suddenly I heard George let out a roar of laughter, and as I stood beside my desk, actually cringing from embarrassment, George said loudly: " 'It's the right answer, Fred, but not for *that* question.' "

George delighted in mischief and pranks. He would often take eggs from the Eggen and Hoyem's Swedish Bake Shop. While talking to people, he would slip the eggs into their pockets and then slap the area when the conversation was over. This left the person with egg yoke inside his clothes.

Gipp spent much of his youth at the Calumet Y.M.C.A. He learned swimming and basketball at the 'Y' and received an introduction to billiards. But, from the time he was ten years old, baseball was his sport. Gipp was much better than players his age, and, according to Lyman Frimodig, a triple letter star at Calumet High School, Gipp had a great love for baseball.

"He always wanted to play with the older boys. And they resented him, partly due to jealousy, I suspect, because of his superior talent. I used to feel sorry for him, and soon after we'd choose up sides, I'd pick George. He was damn good. He just bubbled with enthusiasm. He'd chase foul balls all day long if you'd let him and never complain. He just wanted to play, and he was willing to do anything. You just had to see him for a minute with either a bat or glove to know he was a natural."

In 1908, Gipp won the annual Laurium foot race. In fact, he was so far ahead of any of the others that he was able to stop before he got close to the finish line and wait for the other racers to get close before putting on a final burst of speed which gave him the victory.

Basketball was also a sport where Gipp thrived. In 1910 Gipp became a starter on the Calumet High basketball team that won 24 games in a row.

But, Gipp did not have a long career as a high school athlete. This was because he was unwilling to bring his grades up to the level required for participation in organized sports. In classes that required students to remember facts and figures, Gipp was always having troubles. However, in other classes that required expression Gipp, was able, on occasion, to perform. He displayed a touch of humor in a poem written for a freshman English class:

> *Now there is always a chance for poets to write*
> *Of things that we see and that startle the sight*
> *Of how Beasley went around in his aeroplane true*
> *With his head toward the green and his feet to the blue*
> *Now a picture of this how well I could paint,*
> *If I were a Keats, but you see now I ain't.*
>
> *Now if I were Shelley who also wrote poems*
> *I'd tell of the paths thru the air that he wound,*
> *I'd tell how he soared like a bird on high*
> *While the crowd watched below with a prayer and a sigh.*
> *I'd tell how he saw all the angels and saints*
> *If I were a Keats, but of course now I ain't.*
>
> *Now Gibbon they say wrote a history true*
> *Of things that had happened afore me and you,*
> *Of battles and wars and of wayward sons*
> *Whose only ambition was great battles won,*
> *Of great men I'd tell with their ways so quaint*
> *If I were a Keats and I'm sorry I ain't.*

However, Gipp's scholastic achievements were few and far between. By his senior year Calumet Principal, E.J. Hall, spent most of his time expelling and reinstating Gipp. The last time Gipp was expelled was two weeks before graduation, this time for smoking in the hallway.

There is an attempt among historians to glorify George Gipp. In many of the books written about Gipp, authors have glossed over great periods of Gipp's life. Many have tried to rewrite history to suit a romantic belief that Gipp was smarter than his classmates. But, according to school records and personal accounts which involved recollections of teammates and players who played on the opposite side of the line, Gipp never actually finished Calumet High School. There is no record at Calumet High School of Gipp's graduation. Angelo Stappas, a lifelong friend of Gipp's, said he never graduated. Others have also said that Gipp never received a high school diploma.

By his mid teens, Gipp had found that he liked to play cards and shoot pool more than he liked going to school. When the winter months came around and dumped great amounts of snow on Laurium, Gipp and Stappas would often cut school and spend the day playing cards.

Gambling was a preoccupation with Gipp. It was his great love, perhaps much more than football, baseball or other sports. Gipp seemed to like wagering on games of chance. During his career at Notre Dame, Gipp would find a way to place bets on just about every game. Although, Coach Rockne despised the gambling and the influence professional bettors had on college sports, he was unable to prevent Gipp from having a good relationship with just about every bookie in South Bend.

In his early days in Laurium, Gipp found that gambling provided a good diversion from classes. He would spend days at the poker table, winning money from copper miners. At that time the population of Calumet was nearly 40,000, second only to Detroit. It was a boom town, as the copper industry provided a good living for miners who came from all across the country. Several trains a day came from Chicago, bringing job-seekers who had immigrated from England and Italy. Gipp never really liked the C&H Mining Company. By the time Gipp was in his teens the company had control of just about the entire town. Gipp vowed that he would never work for C&H. Instead, he found employment at Roehm Construction for brief periods of time. He also drove a cab for a couple of years, shuttling people from the train station to The Michigan House and back.

The boom town days were short-lived. In 1912, the copper miners began a battle for unionization. It was a brutal battle that lasted for three years and just about destroyed the copper mining industry in northern Michigan. The main issues in the strike involved wages, the 8-hour day and recognition of the right to unionize. The union organizers came from other states, after successfully organizing miners in several western states.

They encountered stiff resistance from officials of C&H and from workers who saw them as a threat to the community. But eventually the union organizers were able to persuade miners to push for recognition of the union. Eventually a strike was called. The company brought in other workers and tried to reopen the mines. A battle ensued and several people were killed. The governor eventually has to order troops into the area. This battle over unionization divided the town. Gipp was growing up at the time, and he never got involved in the dispute.

When he didn't work at Roehm, Gipp worked as a waiter and as a chauffeur for The Michigan House. He was high-strung, always looking for action. When the town didn't provide enough of a diversion, Gipp and his cronies would invent their own games of chance.

Angelo Stappas related this story about an effort to promote some action:

"...They painted the football white, which he called the 'ghostball' and they would go to the Calumet High School football field after dark, with Italian immigrants who once played soccer in Italy. All the gamblers came one night, following Gipp and Stappas to the field. The Italian kicker would kick a soccer ball and Gipp would kick the football, which in those days was almost as round."

They would begin the contest at the 15-yard line. Angelo would ask Gipp to "take it easy" on the Italians so they would want to keep gambling. So, Gipp would miss while the stakes were low, but when the contest moved farther and farther away from the goalpost the accuracy returned. By the end of the night, Gipp and his friends would often have nearly $100 from ghostball. On several occasions the ghostball contests would go on late into the night. Police would come to chase people away from the field. But Gipp and Stappas would bribe the officers with money to allow the game to continue.

High School Days

When Gipp wasn't gambling or carousing he spent much of his time playing baseball for various company teams. In 1915, Gipp joined a Laurium team that played in the Trolley League, one of the best amateur leagues in Michigan.

Gipp had exceptional talent on the ball-field. He could hit for average and power. As centerfielder he covered as much ground as Ty Cobb and his throwing arm was remarkable. In the summer of 1915, Gipp's team won the Trolley League title. Following the end of the season, Gipp's team was matched up against the winner of another county league. The first two batters in the eighth inning struck out with Gipp's team trailing by a run, the third batter singled to right. Gipp came up and ripped a fastball well over the center field wall. Joe Savinni, a teammate said, "...There was a coal pile well beyond the centerfield area, and that ball was still soaring as it went over it. It was the longest drive ever hit by anybody up here."

One year, towards the end of summer in Northern Michigan, Angelo Stappas invited Gipp to a picnic. After Gipp and his cronies had feasted, they went out on Lake Superior to troll for white fish.

After they had caught a good amount of fish the men headed back. But, a violent storm disrupted things. It capsized the boat as it was nearing the shore. Several of the men managed to stay afloat by clinging to the boat. But another man, who weighed well over 250 pounds couldn't hold on. He slipped away and began to go under. Gipp saw the man heading down and swam over. He pulled him up and was able to swim back to the shore. It was the first time anyone knew that George could swim.

In 1916 Gipp didn't play much baseball. He spent much time at Jimmy O'Brien's Pool Room, which was three blocks from his house on Hecla Street. If the pool room didn't fill his time, Gipp would trolley to The Michigan House in Calumet. For money, Gipp would drive the cab on weekends, ferrying copper miners to and from the bars and the local house of prostitution.

The owner of the house of prostitution once offered to share a percentage of the take with Gipp, but he turned it down. It was a pastime for George Gipp. When the gambling dried up in Calumet, Gipp and Stappas would journey to Chicago and meet up with some of the big-time gamblers. A frequent player with their group was Nick "the Greek", who was perhaps one of the best poker players of his era.

Most of the time was spent playing pool. "He wasn't exactly cocky, but he had no reverence for anybody or anything. He was winning a hell of a lot of money what with poker and pool, but he was throwing it away just as fast as it came to him. He just didn't seem to give a damn about anything," recalled an old friend.

By the end of the summer of 1916, Gipp got an offer to go to Notre Dame and play baseball.

Since 1909, Indiana State Senator Robert Emmett Proctor formed a baseball team of Notre Dame students, the group would barnstorm through the Upper Peninsula.

One year the barnstorming group was having a difficult time winning against the amateur teams of the area. Proctor decided to get some local talent to fill out his team. After some negotiations, Paul Hogan and Wilbur Gray became members of the Notre Dame team.

After the two joined the club the fortunes were reversed. The team won all of its remaining games and Hogan and Gray were offered scholarships to Notre Dame. In 1910, Gray accepted the scholarship and went to Notre Dame, where he was a star for four years until he graduated in 1914. After playing semi-pro ball in Indiana, Gray returned to Laurium in 1916.

One day he ran into Gipp on the street and suggested that Gipp, with his great ability, could easily get a scholarship and go to Notre Dame.

"I'm too old to try school again," George said. "Besides, I don't have any money."

There was also the problem of Gipp's lack of a high school diploma. But, Gray, Hogan and other friends of Gipp persuaded him to give it a shot. A fund-raising drive began, as merchants in the area pitched in to raise money for the train fare. So, in early September, Gipp boarded a train that would take him to South Bend.

Gipp left Laurium with very little money and not much more than the clothes on his back. He told a friend back home, "I was really upset when I got to Notre Dame, mainly on account of I didn't have much money. But they were pretty good about it. And after awhile, everything was jake."

The History of Notre Dame

Notre Dame began as a Catholic mission in 1830 through the effort of Father Stephen T. Badin. Badin came to the area to continue the work of Claude Allouez, a Jesuit priest who had converted the Potawatomi tribe in the late 18th Century.

Within a year Badin has succeeded in building a school and an orphanage. It was a time of growth in the South Bend area, as the parish expanded to a 50-mile block of territory. The growth continued for several years, but, demographic trends were working against the mission. The great westward expansion was in full force by the end of the first decade of the schools operation. In 1838 the mission closed after U.S. troops forced the Potawatomi Indians out. It was a continuation of the policy which pushed Indian tribes further and further west. An eviction notice removed the Indians and for many years the mission remained abandoned.

In 1841, Father Edward Sorin and seven brothers belonging to the Congregation of the Holy Cross began a plan to move into the abandoned mission and build a university. In mid-November of 1842, the group began the journey from Vincennes. It was a long, eleven day journey which ended with a prayer to the Blessed Virgin Mary after the group consecrated the land.

The intervening years had left much of the area a thick forest. Fr. Sorin and the group cleared the land and began their construction. In 1844, after one building was finished, the group was able to get a grant and a charter from the State of Indiana to establish a college.

At its beginning, the University of Notre Dame was not a great institution of higher learning. It was not a Harvard, a Yale, or a Princeton. The mission of the School was to train impoverished boys in the various trades. It was not necessarily a classic university in the sense that its main goal was to allow graduates to survive in the industrial revolution of the 19th century.

The first 50 years of the school remain its most difficult. The biggest problem at that time was finances. Its financial base was weak. But, it struggled through and by the 1870s the school was achieving some moderate success. The school was hit with a series of outbreaks of malaria and in 1879 a fire destroyed several buildings.

Notre Dame was able to survive, and by the beginning of the 20th Century it was one of the best universities in the Midwest, as it was able to change to a more scholastic. The students who attended the school came from Illinois, Indiana, Michigan, Ohio and Wisconsin. For many, it was the first formal education. The school trained doctors, lawyers, businessmen and others. For those who could not afford tuition, the school offered a job plan that allowed the students to work on campus and earn money for tuition. If no jobs were to be found at the school, the administrators often would get businesses in South Bend to hire students. The close relationship between the South Bend business community and the school was established and helped when athletics came to the school.

College football, which first began in the east, came to the Midwest in the 1890s. For Notre Dame, the big sport was baseball. One of the most famous graduates, Cap Anson played at Notre Dame and went on to star with the Chicago Cubs. Anson led the league in hitting in 1887 and 1888 and later guided the team to five National League pennants. Dozens of Notre Dame players made it to the majors after the school began offering baseball as an intramural sport in 1892.

When competitive sport thrived during this time, it was baseball, not football that was the main sport at Notre Dame. The school barnstormed with its teams throughout the Midwest and journeyed east. In 1913, an eastern tour brought games with Pennsylvania, Navy, Fordham, Catholic University, and for the first time ever, a game with Army. This baseball competition set the stage and paved the way for the football competition that was to follow. Jesse Harper, the football coach wrote letters to several of the schools that Notre Dame had played in baseball, asking for a game.

The success of the baseball program led to the success of the football program. It is clear that if Notre Dame didn't have a good baseball program, the football program would never have been established. The barnstorming, the travel and the contacts developed by the baseball coach, William Cutter, allowed the football team to arrange games. Once football was established, baseball just about disappeared as a competitive sport at Notre Dame.

The first baseball game with Army, which Notre Dame won, 3–0, led to a contract for a football game in 1914. By this time, Knute Rockne had begun playing for the Fighting Irish. As the team journeyed to face Army, it was given little chance of victory. But, Rockne and Gus Dorias had a secret plan for Army. After Notre Dame fell behind, 13–0, Dorias began to use the forward pass. It was a move that helped to revolutionize football. Notre Dame won the game, 35–13, and history was made.

When it first began, football was played on an intramural basis. Father John W. Cavanaugh, president of the school, believed that this type of sport helped students thrive at the school. He was convinced that intramural sports, like football and baseball, helped sharpen young men and prepare them for life's struggle. It was not his intention to create a massive sports program, at this time, sports programs were viewed as a money loser for schools. Varsity sports did not make money because there wasn't a well-established market. There was little uniformity and regulation of college sports. Players could leave teams at will and there was little to prevent one player from ditching his school in mid-season when a more attractive offer came along. Cavanaugh enticed Jesse Harper away from his post at nearby Wabash College and Harper began to build the football tradition at Notre Dame.

As athletic director, Harper began the task of improving sports at Notre Dame by establishing an intramural system that exists to this day. By the time George Gipp came to Notre Dame, there were 40 intramural teams competing for titles in various sports. The intramural competition was often fiercer and tougher than games between the Notre Dame varsity and other schools.

Gipp's Arrival

George Gipp arrived on the Notre Dame campus in mid-September, 1916. Gipp took up residence at Brownson Hall. He also joined the football team for a few days, but quit after he found it boring.

Gipp did not like student life. He appeared restless and was out-of-place with the rest of the students. He was three years older than most of them and generally kept to himself. A friend who remembered Gipp said that during the first few weeks he "wasn't the easiest person to get to know."

Coach Rockne wrote that Gipp was quiet and low key during the first few weeks of school. "He stayed mostly to himself, lived quietly, and had few friends. He was pleasant without being cheerful, affable without being congenial. He appeared just too sure of himself," Rockne wrote.

Another friend of Gipp's, Walter Miller, recalled that Gipp spent much time playing pool in the school recreation room during his first few months. "I remember seeing him come into the recreation room quite often. he was always alone. He'd spend maybe an hour or two shooting pool all by himself. I used to enjoy watching him shoot pool as he could really handle a cue stick. As I remember, it was nothing for him to run off upwards of eighty balls without a miss. All the times I saw him do this I don't recall his ever saying as much as two words to anybody."

Gipp was involved in classes. He had a full workload, including classes in English, history, biology, political science and German. While he attended most of the class sessions, friends have maintained that he sat in the back of the room and did not take much interest in the classroom discussion.

The classroom was an obstacle to many students at Notre Dame who played on its athletic teams. By this time the football team was a good source of revenue for the school and pressure was exerted to keep players eligible. There was also opposing pressure to maintain high academic standards. A faculty board had oversight authority with the sports teams. There was a constant battle between Coach Rockne and Athletic Director Harper on one side and school administrators on the other to maintain credibility. Several players went through periods where they were suspended and reinstated. During his career at Notre Dame this happened to Gipp on more than one occasion.

In his book, *A History of Notre Dame Football*, author Jim Beach included a letter written by Gipp shortly after he began at Notre Dame. The letter revealed that Gipp was depressed about things at Notre Dame. The atmosphere was confining and Gipp wanted to recapture some of the fun he had in Laurium.

"I got here alright and got away with a pretty good start. Not so much my fault as the school's — I'm in a mood tonight where I'd like to go straight up. I want to come and go as I please. Sometimes I wonder what I'm here for. For a while I felt decidedly human. But I can't seem to shake this recurring grouch I've got. It isn't a grouch exactly but it's something that makes me feel that I'm all wrong and will stay that way. I don't think that I'm not trying hard to get rid of it. Tonight is the first time that I've felt like this since I've been down here. I'd like to give up and quit right now, chuck everything and go anywhere."

But, Gipp decided to stick it out. One day, late in September he was fooling around in front of Brownson Hall, kicking a football with his friends. In an article for *Collier's Weekly*, Rockne recalled his first meeting with Gipp.

I first met George Gipp on a football field. It was and is a habit of mine to stroll to the practice field and observe groups of freshmen or nondescript students kicking footballs around. Once in a great while you can spot, among these clumsy beginners, genuine talent.

On one early autumn afternoon in 1916 the practice field was all but deserted. A tall lad in everyday campus clothes was booting a football to a boy in a playing suit who kicked it back. The uniformed lad was a candidate for the freshman team. Their play seemed nothing more than the usual duet of punts between a football aspirant and some hall friend or roommate who had come out to oblige. The style of the taller boy (Gipp) caught my eye. He picked up the ball, poised his body with natural grace, slid the ball to the ground, and drop-kicked with perfect ease —fifty yards. For about ten minutes I watched him. His kicks were far and placed where he wanted them to go to give the other player catching practice. Here, I thought, was somebody worth examining. When he strolled from the field as if bored, I stopped him.

"What's your name?" I asked.

Most freshmen regard the football coach as if he's a deity on duty for the season. This boy was almost indifferent. "Gipp," he said, "George Gipp. I come from Laurium, Michigan."

"Played high school football?" I asked.

"No," he said, "don't particularly care for football. Baseball's my game."

"What led you to come to Notre Dame?" I asked.

"Friends of mine are here," he said.

"Put on a football suit tomorrow," I invited, "and come out with the freshmen scrubs. I think you'll make a football player."

The lad with Gipp stared pop-eyed.

"Why," he said, "He's kicking those punts and drops with ordinary low shoes. What'll he do with football boots?"

Rockne Discovers Gipp

The next day Gipp came to the practice field and began practicing and scrimmaging with the freshman team. The equipment manager gave him football shoes that were worn by Bay Eichenlaub, a great football player who played at Notre Dame from 1910 through 1914.

The very first time Gipp touched the ball he rumbled through the freshman line for a touchdown. For the next month, Gipp drilled with the freshman team. During this time his skills improved greatly. His passing was pin-point, and he drop-kicked and punted with the skill of a varsity player. Coach Rockne, who at the time, was an assistant under Jesse Harper came up with the plan he thought would allow Notre Dame to beat Army.

The main star of the Army team was Elmer Q. Oliphant, who had previously starred at Purdue University before transferring to the Academy. A great baseball player, Oliphant was similar to Gipp in ability. He was widely acknowledged as the best ball carrier of his time. An opponent once said of Oliphant: "Trying to stop a charging Oliphant was equivalent to standing in front of a speeding locomotive, and just about as foolhardy."

To train for Army, Rockne used Gipp to mimic plays that Army ran. He got Gipp to copy Oliphant's running style, which involved veering and a great deal of changes in running direction. Rockne wrote that Gipp was exceedingly patient, and that by the end of the three days of practice, Gipp was able to give a perfect imitation of the Army star.

On November 3, 1816 the freshmen opened their season against St. Viator's. Gipp saw his first action in the third quarter and helped Notre Dame to a 10–7 victory with a long drop-kick.

The next day Notre Dame faced Army. The defense was primed to stop Oliphant, but, it didn't even come close. Army won, 30–10, and Oliphant ran wild. After he was confronted by a reporter, Rockne said, "The only drawback was that in the game, Oliphant gave a perfect imitation of Gipp."

The next week the Notre Dame freshman team journeyed to Kalamazoo, Michigan to play Western State Normal (which is now Western Michigan University). By this time Gipp had been appointed captain.

It was a brutal game. Notre Dame and Western State Normal battled to a 7–7 tie late into the fourth quarter. Gipp had scored the only Notre Dame touchdown, and had been responsible for 174 of the 216 total yards Notre Dame gained.

Time was running out on Notre Dame and they faced a fourth and long at their own 38-yard line. Quarterback Frank Thomas called for a punt; it seemed like the safest choice. It was certainly the most prudent. But

Gipp didn't want to settle for a tie. "Why settle for a tie?" Gipp said, "Let me try a drop kick."

"Forget it, just punt the ball," Thomas said.

Gipp dropped back into punt formation and Western State Normal braced for a punt. Walter Olsen, the safety, dropped back and prepared for the punt. "I had caught a couple of 50-yard punts of Gipp's during the game, so naturally I was plenty far back, figuring it was another punt. The ball came through the air like a line drive in baseball and to my surprise it went sailing over the crossbar for the three points that beat us 10–7."

It was a bitter loss for Western State. Warren Allen, who had just entered the game, said it was difficult to accept. "I was sent in at right tackle to try to block what we all expected was going to be a punt. I remember that it was a low kick that went right between the goal posts, which were situated right on the goal line in those days. This was our first loss in five years and it really rocked our prestige. It has a hard loss to take."

In his book, *A History of Notre Dame Football*, Jim Beach wrote that the kick left many on the field confused.

"At the snap from center Irish end Dave Hayes checked the opposing tackle for an instant and then sprinted downfield. He headed straight for the safety man and was shocked to see the Western State player (Olsen) turn his back. Dave was confused for a moment, and then wondered why the crowd was cheering.

"What happened?" Hayes asked.

"The sonofagun drop-kicked."

As years would go by, the 62-yard drop kick would remain one of the longest in history. To this day, it is the second longest drop-kick in the history of football.

The important thing about the drop-kick is that it was much more difficult than to kick a simple field goal. It involved sliding the ball to the ground and then kicking it. The art disappeared because it became much more reliable to have a man place the ball and hold it up. Today's football has pointed ends.

When drop-kicking was used it appeared as an outgrowth of soccer. The pointed ends of the modern football made it much easier to pass, but also more difficult to drop-kick. Sometime during the 1940s coaches began relying on the straight ahead field goal kick, which involved the center, the placement man and the kicker.

After the kick, Gipp came back to the campus as a hero. But, it didn't seem to affect him a great deal. He was soon back to his old habits, pool and poker.

The First Season

The Notre Dame freshman team finished its three game schedule against the Kalamazoo College freshman team by losing 34–7. Notre Dame's only score came on a long touchdown run by Gipp.

Despite the new attention and stardom, Gipp remained aloof. A fellow team member said, "George never let his play go to his head. I don't remember him displaying even a hint of condescension in his relations with me, or with any other player for that matter."

When school let out for Christmas break, Gipp returned home to be with his family. During his vacation he played pool and poker, and won a lot of money which he gave much away to poor people.

Gipp also spent a great deal of time hunting during his trips back home to Northern Michigan. During deer season Gipp and Angelo Stappas made several trips running moonshine to Hurley, Wisconsin, a small town then known for its rough saloons and rougher girls of the evening. One day they spotted a large buck, nearly 200 yards away. Angelo told Gipp to get in a prone position and take a shot at the buck. Just when he was ready to shoot, two fawns appeared alongside the buck and Gipp froze. He couldn't pull the trigger. Many beginning hunters had the same problem, known in the North Country as 'buck fever.'

"This is the first sport I have ever failed at," Gipp said, "I sure am chicken," and he put down his rifle.

The two continued their journey to Hurley. With a load of whiskey in the back seat both were fearful that the state police would confiscate the load. Angelo told George to pretend he was asleep when they approached the town. As they arrived near the outskirts, the state police stopped their car but when the officer saw Gipp sleeping in the back seat, he waved them on.

"We sure were lucky to get by without having to go through the inspection," said Stappas.

"Hell no, I was just a good actor," Gipp replied.

During winter months Gipp spent the most enjoyable periods of his life. Calumet was usually snow-bound by December, but that didn't stop Gipp from getting around. George taxied miners through the town with a horse drawn carriage, often supplying them with a bottle of whiskey during the trip.

Stappas often sent Gipp $75 a month while he was at Notre Dame. Gipp told Rockne about 220 pound Stappas and recommended him for a scholarship. But Stappas was reluctant about leaving the fun and games: "But George, if we both go to school, who in is going to support us, especially the life style we enjoy. I have to stay back here and gamble so I can send you money."

Gipp continued to get extra money monthly from Angelo. When Stappas had a run of bad luck, he was always able to get cash from James Gekas, the author's father.

When it came time to return to South Bend, Gipp told his friends that he was quitting school because he didn't have enough money for the trip. Again, merchants and others took up a collection for the train ticket.

"As soon as it was learned George was short the money for a train ticket, all of his friends got together and took up a collection for him. When we got enough collected, we went over to the depot in Calumet and bought his ticket. Later, when we made him a present of it, I detected in his attitude that he was a bit disappointed... at the time he was quite disillusioned with college life," said baseball teammate Joe Savinni.

When Gipp got back to South Bend he started working out with the basketball team. He toyed briefly with the track team and in the spring began his baseball career. Gipp originally came to Notre Dame to play baseball, yet he only played one game with the team. In the late innings of his first game the manager instructed Gipp to bunt. Instead, Gipp swung away and hit a towering home run. Afterwards, Gipp said, "It's too hot today to run bases." The next day he turned in his uniform and quit the baseball team.

At the end of March, Gipp and other freshmen football players started spring practice. On April 3rd, an exhibition game was staged between the freshman team and a team composed of Notre Dame alumni including Knute Rockne, who played quarterback. Gipp and his team lost, 14–7, but the coaches were exceedingly happy with the game. Gipp displayed some sharp passing and the coaches thought Notre Dame would go undefeated during the next season.

But, world events intruded on the plans for the 1917 football season. Following the sinking of the Lusitania, President Woodrow Wilson called for a declaration of war on Germany. Congress passed draft bill and millions of men were enlisted. Gipp was not drafted, instead, he spent the summer playing baseball for the local team. After a game in September, the local Laurium Draft Board announced that Gipp had been drafted. Yet, when the South Shore passenger train left the Copper Country area for the Army post at Battle Creek, Michigan, Gipp was nowhere to be seen.

Notre Dame officials thought that Gipp was in the Army, until he arrived on campus after the season's second game — a 0–0 tie against Wisconsin. What Gipp did between the Laurium baseball game and his arrival at Notre Dame is not known. One account places him in Kenosha playing for a semi-pro baseball team. In *The History of Notre Dame Football*, author Jim Beach recalls that Knute Rockne went to Kenosha to get Gipp.

"...Rock had a deep-rooted affection for George, and he thought as highly of the boy's intelligence as he did of his athletic ability. Gipp resisted Rockne's usual psychological devices and laughed-off the coach's petulant sarcasm. Rock dealt with George by being completely straightforward. The result was a unique rapport: 'We need you in the backfield, George,' "

"Since you put it that way, Rock, when does the next train leave?" Gipp asked.

It is clear that Gipp, from the time he missed the train to Battle Creek to join the Army, until the game against Morningside on November 10th was technically a "draft dodger". His health was good, he was within the draft age and he should have served in the Army.

Angelo Stappas, a close friend, said Gipp wasn't afraid of war. "He just didn't like the regimentation," Stappas said. "He could care less for uniforms."

Gipp came back on the day after the Wisconsin game. He played in four games during the 1917 season. The first, against Nebraska turned out to be Notre Dame's only loss of the season. Because of Gipp's late arrival, he was unable to play in the starting line-up. It was one of the few times that Gipp did not start. From the beginning, the Nebraska game was a tough, brutal battle. Gipp's absence from the starting line-up hurt Notre Dame's offense. Notre Dame scored 55 points in a romp over Kalamazoo to begin the season on October 6th, but hadn't scored a point since. Against Nebraska the defense dominated. Early in the second quarter a long sustained drive left the Cornhuskers on the Notre Dame one-yard line.

Hugo Otopalik, a big, tough Nebraska back who later became the coach of the U.S. Olympic Wrestling Team, took a hand-off and dived over for the only score of the game. The Notre Dame offense couldn't move and late in the third quarter, Gipp entered the game. On one of his first plays, he broke away for a 30-yard run that put the ball on the Cornhuskers' 10-yard line. However, on the next play, Nebraska intercepted the ball and killed off Notre Dame's only chance for a score.

The next week Gipp was back in the starting line-up for a game against South Dakota. It was to be the only home appearance by Gipp in the 1917 season. Notre Dame won in a romp, 40–0. While Gipp had several long runs against South Dakota, he is remembered most for his defensive play. Carl Hoy, the center for South Dakota remembered Gipp as a great defensive player. "He would knock you down with a vicious tackle and then, after helping you up, apologize for hitting you so hard," Hoy said.

The next week, on November 3rd, Notre Dame faced the Army Cadets at West Point. In 1916, Army ruined Notre Dame's chance for a perfect season with a 30–10 victory. Gipp emulated Army star Elmer Q. Oliphant in the practice sessions for this game. In the 1917 Army game, Gipp had a starring role.

It was a long, brutal defensive struggle. Army trapped Notre Dame in the end-zone in the first half and the two-point safety held up until late in the fourth quarter. With about five minutes remaining, quarterback Joe Brandy engineered a drive that worked its way to the Army five-yard line. The Army defense braced itself for an off-tackle play by Gipp, but, instead Brandy faked to Gipp and walked into the end-zone unmolested.

But Army wasn't finished. Late in the game the cadets drove deep into Notre Dame territory. On fourth down, the drive petered-out and Army set up for a field goal that would cut the lead to two points. Right before the play began Gipp alerted his teammates to a fake. Gipp was able to do it and knocked the attempted pass down. It saved the game for Notre Dame.

After the game, the Associated Press blamed Army's defeat on the war. "Notre Dame outclassed Army in every department. They are better coached and better finished. Their shift completely confused the Army line. Only in punting did Army have an edge. However,

Army is handicapped by a shortage of coaches due to the war. The material on hand is good, but, the men are limited to only one practice session per week."

Several Notre Dame players were missing from the game; quarterback Jim Phelan was drafted before the Army game, and others were missing. For the two years of the war, football was plagued by player depletion and the postponement of games. Scheduled games were often changed at the last minute, as travel restrictions cut into athletic activities. The players that remained were often underclassmen and those who didn't have the ability of the players that went into the U.S. Army.

Following the two wins, Notre Dame traveled to Sioux City, Iowa, to face Morningside College. This game was to be a breather on the Notre Dame schedule. It was common practice for Notre Dame and other schools with good football programs to book games with decidedly inferior opponents. Notre Dame could fatten up on the schedule and raise interest for other, more substantial games. The game with Morningside was viewed as a pushover.

But, Morningside did not view it that way. It came to the contest with an undefeated record, led by Jerry Johnson, a fast halfback who ran the 100 in ten seconds.

For George Gipp, the Morningside game was over quickly. On the first play from scrimmage, Gipp took a hand-off and sped around the right end. The line opened a big hole and Gipp had 35 yards of clear sailing. He was knocked out of bounds by two Morningside players and crashed into a steel fence post. The force of the collision caused a broken ankle and knocked Gipp out of the game and ended his season.

Horace Wulf was one of the players involved in the play. He and Vic Menafee, a lineman ran Gipp out of bounds. We both hit him at the same time and he spun around, his leg hitting a fence post that had been temporarily installed for the game. While he lay on the ground I said to him, "I'm sorry, boy, I hope it isn't bad," he replied, "Forget it, pal, you had to come in. It's all in the game."

The Notre Dame offense ran out of steam after Gipp left the game. In fact, mistakes by Morningside led to all of Notre Dame's points in their 13–0 victory. The first touchdown came in the second quarter as an intercepted pass was returned for a touchdown. A fumble in the third quarter gave Notre Dame its second touchdown.

The Marooners of Morningside outgained Notre Dame by 150 yards, but every time they neared scoring, a mistake, a penalty, or an infraction set them back.

Gipp spent 11 days in St. Vincent's Hospital where physicians told him that he was finished for the year. While the rest of the team went on to finish with victories against Michigan State and Washington & Jefferson, Gipp spent the last half of 1917 in a depressed state. One day after he returned to South Bend, he dropped out of school.

The leg injury provided Gipp with a reason to avoid the Army. In January, he was ordered to report for a physical examination by the Laurium Draft Board. On January 31st he reported. At that time, according to Hunk Anderson, a teammate, Gipp was still limping noticeably. He was given a six-month deferment.

The Summer of 1918

Gipp didn't return to Notre Dame until September of 1918. He spent the summer playing pool, gambling and baseball. His leg was healing, and soon he was his old self again. It was a joyous summer.

When Gipp and his friends got bored, they went to Chicago for gambling. He ran into Frank "Titanic" Thomas and lost some money trying to throw a ball through a tenth story window. By time the summer ended, Gipp was ready to go back to Notre Dame. But, he wanted to take his friends with him.

Hunk Anderson remembered how Gipp recruited him to play for Notre Dame.

"I can well remember the hot summer day Gipp, Ojay, and Gray came over, armed with the Notre Dame yearbook, *The Dome*, and how they gave me the old sales pitch. Thumbing through the pages, I noted the profusion of clergy."

"Is this place Catholic?" I queried Gipp, although I knew it was.

"Yeah," Gipp replied. "Just remember... when in Rome, do as the Romans do."

"It's a good school," Ojay chimed in, trying to reassure me.

"Tell you what," said Gipp. "When we get back, I'll talk to Rockne and I'll get you fixed up."

Later, Gipp bumped into an old high school pal, Frederic Larson, who planned to enlist into the Army, but Gipp was able to persuade him to go to Notre Dame.

"Come down to Notre Dame and play football," George said. "If we don't kill you by the time the season is over, then join the Army."

When Gipp arrived for the fall season, Knute Rockne had taken over from Jesse Harper as head coach of the football team. Harper had left Notre Dame because of a death in his family and now Rockne had total control of awarding scholarships and running Notre Dame athletics.

But, 1918 was a very bad season for football. The best players were taken by the Army. Gipp was able to avoid Army service a second time by joining the Student Army Training Corps (SATC), which allowed college students to train for the military yet remain on their college campuses for education. Among college athletes, the SATC was a "socially acceptable" way to avoid military service.

For Rockne, Gipp's ability to avoid Army service was fortunate. Practically the entire first string team of 1917 was fighting in the war. Gipp had been held out of a lot of the action in 1917 and Rockne was counting on him to provide a spark for the fall season.

Shortly after Gipp arrived at Notre Dame he was able to get a scholarship for Hunk Anderson. Anderson's first meeting with Coach Rockne was quite memorable.

"When I arrived at the old Grand Trunk depot in South Bend, Gipp and Larson were there to meet me. Gipp said that Rockne was having lunch at Hullie and Mike's and would be by shortly. I was to discover later that Hullie and Mike's was the downtown hangout for Notre Dame students, chiefly because of the good food served at the counter in generous portions and at reasonable prices. The establishment also placed bets on Notre Dame games for the students, and the back room served as a pool hall and poker parlor."

"We didn't wait but a couple of minutes when Rock appeared. Gipp introduced me."

"Coach, this is Hunk Anderson, the fellow I was telling you about."

"Rockne greeted me with an unintelligible salutation, taking a toothpick out of his mouth and shifting a cigar over to that side. He looked me square in the eye and then up and down as though he were judging a steer for the blue ribbon prize at a county fair."

"What position do you play?" inquired Rockne.

"Fullback."

"Fullback? We don't need fullbacks," countered Rockne, "we need guards."

"Well, you're looking at the best guard you'll ever see," I replied confidently.

"I hope so," said Rock. "Of course, if you have the natural ability that George says you have... we can teach you."

"You won't have to teach me very much. I know a little bit about that guard position," I answered.

Rockne was trying hard to hide a grin. I saw him wink at Gipp as he departed with a "see ya on campus."

Rockne had some serious problems as he readied the team for the 1918 season. Much of the team was Army rejects and freshmen. For Gipp, Anderson and others in the Student Army Training Corps, it was a difficult period. They had to get up at 5:30 a.m. and drill for nearly two hours before classes began. Gipp stayed with the program for a few weeks, but when the football season began in earnest he dropped out.

On September 17th, Rockne held the first workout.

The *South Bend Tribune* reported that the Gold and Blue were a little "green". "...Twenty Gold and Blue gridiron candidates trotted out for the first official practice of the season yesterday and were greeted by a field of mud and drizzle. Bahan and Gipp were the only two regulars to report for initial duty and Hogan was the only ex-freshman warrior to show up.

"*Green* is the one word to describe the material for the Gold and Blue eleven this season so far as can be seen just now. Not that the youngsters do not know any football at all, or that they are an awkward squad. Some of them look quite promising, but they have a long way to go to measure up to traditional varsity standards."

At other colleges around the midwest, teams barely had enough players to field a team. At the University of Minnesota only 13 players turned out for the first practice session. The University of Chicago football team was composed of "last years freshmen" and part of the baseball team.

Notre Dame opened its season against Case Tech of Ohio on September 28th. On the day of the game the U.S. War Department issued an order banning football games where teams had to travel at night. This restriction decimated Notre Dame's October football games. In effect, it meant that the school would only be able to play schools in the nearby area.

Case opened the scoring in the first quarter, with a good running attack. Shortly after Case took a 6–0 lead, Gipp and Bahan took control of the game. After the start of the second quarter, running by Gipp and Bahan brought the ball close, and Lambeau crashed over the line tying the score. Gipp scored two touchdowns in the third quarter and Notre Dame was never behind again; winning 26–6. Gipp did not play a full game, as he entered the contest after Notre Dame fell behind. It is believed that his foot was still hurting. Coach Rockne was happy with the effort, but disappointed by some of the play. "When the team lined up Saturday for the Case game, Notre Dame put the lightest team in its history on the field," Rockne said after the game. "The team as a whole was ragged, nevertheless, this team, despite its light weight has all the spirit and fight that any of the older and heavier teams had. The great asset of this year's team is its fighting spirit, which never lagged all during the game Saturday."

Rockne had special praise for Gipp and Bahan. "Bahan and Gipp, of course, played the real old-time game, and it was due to their hard and consistent work that as large a score was piled up against Case. The line is notably weak. The chief failure they showed in the Case game was a weakness in blocking and tackling, especially the former," Rockne said.

William Edwards, a Case lineman, said Gipp was especially difficult to stop. "He furnished the necessary offensive strength to win the game. He was very powerful, a fast runner who made good use of his interference. And he could run to the right or left equally well. The only way to tackle him was from the blind side. I found the best way was to grab hold of his uniform and hang on until help came along," Edwards said.

As for Gipp, the next month was spent studying. He switched his major from arts to law. Rockne said he didn't care about the switch as long as he studied, but Gipp was developing a bad reputation for classroom work. For him there too many diversions to his main pursuits; playing pool and poker. Gipp began to cut classes, but, his ability on the football field allowed Notre Dame officials to overlook his neglect of academics.

There was no football in October. A wave of influenza hit the Midwest at this time and public meetings and sporting events were cancelled. The October 12th game was put off because of the war. The Kalamazoo team was inducted into the Student Army Training Corps (SATC) on the day of the game. A game, against Purdue, set for October 19th, was also cancelled because of travel restrictions.

Coach Rockne set up games with teams from Army bases, but another influenza epidemic caused cancellations of these games. He eventually set up a game with Nebraska on November 2nd, but this was pushed back because the Lincoln city council voted to keep the ban on sporting events although state officials had allowed continuation of athletic contests. At long last, Rockne arranged a game against Wabash College on November 2nd.

The game was arranged on the Friday night before the contest. At five a.m. the Notre Dame team boarded a train for Crawfordsville to face the small Indiana school. The game itself was no contest. Notre Dame scored early and often and emerged a 67–7 victor. Gipp had a field day.

John Ott, a Wabash defender said Gipp was very difficult to stop. "We were badly outclassed. My job was to dive into the interference and grab legs. I may have laid a hand on Gipp once or twice, but that was all," Ott said.

Gipp was disinterested in the contest. He was only able to get enthused for games that provided a challenge. As soon as Notre Dame got a two touchdown lead, Gipp didn't even want to play. It was common practice for him to take himself out of the game anytime he got bored. He spent most of the second half of the Wabash game on the bench.

The following week Notre Dame faced an excellent team from the Great Lakes Naval Training Center. During these years, the service teams had all the advantages. All of the best players, from all over the country were available to them, while other schools had to struggle with players that were left over. It was inequitable, and many coaches complained about the unfairness. Hunk Anderson wrote that many professional players were on the Navy team. "They had a solid group of ex-collegians led by George Halas and Paddy Driscoll."

Despite the long odds, Rockne was able to get the best from his team. The game ended in a 7–7 tie that many observers viewed as a moral victory for Notre Dame.

The best account of the game came from *The South Bend Tribune.* "...The Great Lakes went into the game with all the advantages known in football. Their line outweighed Notre Dame's by ten pounds to the man. Their backfield had (Paddy) Driscoll, who was picked for the All-American team last year and is considered one of the best all-around backs in the West. Notre Dame had only three veterans, Gipp and Bahan, in the backfield and Rollo Stine in the line.

Gipp spearheaded a long first quarter drive by scoring a touchdown on his favorite off-tackle play. The half ended with the score still in Notre Dame's favor. But Stine was hurt right before half-time and as Notre Dame took the field with "the Great Lakes looking a little the better in condition."

After a few plays Stine had to leave the game. He was the best defensive lineman for Notre Dame and his substitute had a tough time. "His sub found it rough going when Paddy hit the attack right at him," wrote Hunk Anderson. A 35-yard touchdown run by Driscoll tied the score.

Rockne moved Anderson in to play tackle after the score. But, Notre Dame was unable to generate any offense and the game ended in a tie.

Coach Rockne was happy with the effort. "I am satisfied with the game. We went into the game like underdogs and gave them a good fight. The game shows we have as good a team as any in the West," Rockne said.

A week after the game against Great Lakes, Notre Dame put its undefeated record on the line against Michigan (now known as Michigan State). The day before the game a heavy rain fell on the field. On game day the temperatures rose and the field was muddy. This gave the Aggies a great advantage. In addition, Gipp and Bahan were injured early in the second quarter and Stine re-injured his leg.

Gipp was hit in the face and sustained a broken blood vessel that forced him to leave the field. "After we lost Gipp we were ineffective. We could have won if he were able to play the whole game," wrote Hunk Anderson.

The South Bend Tribune said the score would have been worse were it not for the effort of Notre Dame's second string men. "...The outcome of the game once more proves the foresight of Coach Rockne. While local fans were all expecting a victory over the Michigan men, Rockne kept reiterating that the Aggies are a strong and heavy team, and that, though Purdue defeated them, they made ten times as many first downs as did Purdue. And Rockne showed that he meant what he said, for he drilled his lighter team in aerial attack in preference to the frontal, because he knew that the Aggies' line was heavier and stronger than his own. But the best laid schemes of mice and men can go astray, and a wet sloshy field made it impossible for Rockne to use the attack he had prepared, and made useless his plans to depend on speed."

"The Aggies weighed about five pounds more per man than did Rockne's squad, and the score against Notre Dame would have been worse, considering the sloppy condition of the field, were it not for the fight the Indiana men put up continuously. In the fourth quarter, with a whole bunch of second string men,

Notre Dame took the ball right down the field to the Aggies ten yard line only to lose it on a penalty."

The Notre Dame defense played well, but a long touchdown pass gave the Aggies a 13–7 victory. Gipp gained only 52 yards in 15 carries. It was one of the worst games of his career.

On November 23rd, Notre Dame journeyed to Lafayette to face Purdue. Gipp had a great game, rushing for 137 yards in 19 carries, and led Notre Dame to a 26–6 win that gave Notre Dame the State title. *The South Bend Tribune* called Gipp the "tower of strength in Notre Dame's offense, as he tore holes through the Purdue line."

"With the war now over, as the Armistice Agreement was signed on November 11th, teams were free to travel again. Notre Dame was then able to journey to Nebraska to face the Cornhuskers. In 1917, Nebraska ruined Notre Dame's undefeated season by a 7–0 win. But this time Notre Dame appeared to have all the advantages. Its offense was finally in gear and Nebraska was missing many of its key players. But the Cornhuskers played a conservative defensive game. It ended in a 0–0 tie.

"Nebraska fought with the single idea of keeping the visitors from the home goal with the realization that the odds were against it. Ever on the alert for a slip, a fumble or an intercepted pass, and mistake to be turned into an advantage, Nebraska on the whole was playing not so much to score as to keep the other team from scoring. It was smart football, and although it did not win, it kept the other side from winning."

Notre Dame had two scoring opportunities, a fumble and a penalty ruined both of them. In the third quarter Notre Dame drove to the Nebraska 20-yard line before fumbling the ball away. In the fourth quarter, Norm Barry and Johnny Mohardt led the team into the end zone but a touchdown run was called back by the referee, who called a penalty for illegal use of hands. The referee claimed that Barry, in making the touchdown run, had hung onto the back of one of his blockers as he crossed the goal line.

Gipp played in the Nebraska game, but he developed a sore throat in the third quarter and had to leave the game. Hunk Anderson said Notre Dame would have won if Gipp had been able to play the entire game.

The 1918 season ended with three wins, one loss and two ties. For George Gipp, it was a good season. He was able to establish himself as the main star on the Notre Dame team. But injuries prevented him from realizing his full potential this season. Because the quality of football was diminished early, the 1918 football season was viewed as a bust.

However, there was hope for the next season. Veteran players who had been forced into the Army would be returning and Coach Rockne expected to put up a formidable team in 1919. For George Gipp, the next year would establish him as the premier running back in the country.

Winter and Spring, 1919

By the end of the 1818 football season, Gipp had proved himself to be the most valuable player on the Notre Dame team. So important was Gipp, that Coach Rockne started bending team rules to keep Gipp happy. In addition, Notre Dame school officials began bending their academic rules and the rules of personal conduct to keep Gipp at the school. It was unseemly for a school like Notre Dame, which was trying to establish itself as a center for learning and academic achievement, to have a player that delighted in gambling and keeping late hours at nightclubs. Coach Rockne knew there was little he could do to curb Gipp's excesses.

Many viewed the period between 1919 and 1930 as the establishment of a "Golden Era" of Notre Dame. This was due to the great rise in the popularity of football. When Knute Rockne began coaching the Notre Dame football team in 1918, newspaper accounts placed the largest crowd at 10,000. By the end of the 1930 season attendance for games against Army, Southern Cal and other schools had risen to 70,000, reaching more than 120,000 for the first time in a game at the Los Angeles Coliseum in 1927. The increased gate meant increased profits for the Notre Dame athletic department and the school itself. Income from football had moved the schools finances from "shaky" ground in the early days to highly profitable in the last three years Knute Rockne coached the team.

As Gipp emerged as a big star, Notre Dame began to see the potential profits. So, needless to say, football replaced academics as the most important thing on the Notre Dame campus. Football had moved from being a recreational activity for young men to being a business. The college game of the early 1900s became the professional game. Without regulation and without standards, schools could keep anyone on the roster. The loose standards allowed colleges to keep fielding players who should have graduated.

There was a system of "free agency". If a player became dissatisfied with conditions at one school or if the academic standards became too tough, the player could enroll at another school and continue playing football. School officials recognized this, but they overlooked academic inadequacies in order to satisfy the balance sheet. Today's school officials may stand back and say they are "shocked" at these practices, but many of today's them are doing the same things.

Gipp was the type of player that deserved special treatment. He had switched his major from Arts to Law at the beginning of the 1918 academic season, but by the end of the fall semester his grades had slipped. When the rest of the team returned to South Bend after the Nebraska game, Gipp, Hunk Anderson and Ojay Larson spent a few days in Lincoln playing poker and shooting pool. The three missed the last two weeks of classes and began the journey back to Calumet.

Hunk Anderson recalled that the three took a train and headed home with gambling winnings and contraband. "...That Christmas, Ojay Larson, Gipp and I were going to spend the holidays at home. Gipp had won some money gambling and he bought two suitcases full of whiskey for resale when he arrived at Calumet. Because of the war, the railroads had set up inspection stations to search for contraband, and on a stop at one such station, the Grand Trunk Line inspectors boarded our train. When one inspector spotted Gipp's suitcases stuffed under our seat and asked what was in them. He answered, 'Just our clothes.' I thought he might ask us to get them out and open them up, but fortunately he went on to the next seat down the aisle. Gipp sold the booze at a profit of several hundred dollars."

Back in Laurium, Gipp was able to win more money shooting pool. He gave some of the excess to women who lost husbands during the war, but, for the most part whatever he won, he would lose the next night shooting dice. He had a fascination with dice, but not much skill. Though Gipp loved to gamble he didn't do too well in games he couldn't control. He began to focus his betting only on games that he could determine the outcome, like pool and football.

After the Christmas break Gipp returned to Notre Dame for the winter and spring semester. This was an opportunity for Gipp to redeem himself in the classroom and boost his grades. But, after a few weeks of classes, Gipp became bored with student life. He started cutting classes and started hanging out at Hullie and Mike's and the Oliver Hotel.

Gipp ran into a Chicago pool shark known as "the Greek" and won several hundred dollars from him. After this, the two men began keeping steady company. Soon, gamblers from all over the midwest journeyed to South Bend in order to get close to Gipp. In May, Gipp represented Hullie and Mike's in a billiards tournament against the Oliver Hotel. After winning, Gipp was recognized as one of the top pool players in the area.

All of this activity disturbed Notre Dame school officials. By the end of the spring semester Gipp was barely attending one class a week. There was just too much action in downtown South Bend. Gipp skipped his final exams and the faculty had enough. The great George Gipp was expelled from Notre Dame in May, 1919.

During the last two weeks in May, Gipp was establishing himself as a pool player. He was taking on all comers. A pool player from Mishawaka named Ray Fisher came and challenged Gipp. Fisher was a great pool player, and a match set for May 21st attracted a great deal of attention. *The South Bend Tribune* reported that, "...The 100-point pocket billiards match between our George Gipp and Ray Fisher will be watched with interest by local players. It promises to be a keen rivalry, and many local pool experts and fans plan to make the trip to Mishawaka to witness the match."

Fisher had insisted that the first match be held on his home ground, and, to the shock of many, he defeated Gipp. But, the next night, Gipp was able to defeat Fisher and after this he was recognized as the top pool player in the state.

The 1919 Football Season

Notre Dame's 1919 football season marked a return of many players that had served in the Army during World War I. Knute Rockne was firmly in charge of the program and he was optimistic because the returning players would supplement a team that had many problems. Three important players from the 1918 team that compiled a 3–1–2 record wouldn't return. They included, Ojay Larson, Bill Mohn and lineman Rollo Stine. Larson, who had been a close friend of Gipp's was forced to return home to Michigan because of family financial problems. Stine had never really recovered from a leg injury sustained in the game against the Great Lakes Naval Training team. His absence on the line caused problems for Rockne, who spent much of the fall wondering how he would put together his 1919 team.

Despite the loss of the three, Notre Dame still had formidable team. It had perhaps the best backfield talent in the country and, as Coach Rockne led his team out for the first practice, optimism abounded on the Notre Dame campus.

During these years, two major papers covered the Notre Dame football team on a day-to-day basis, the *South Bend Tribune* and *The South Bend Times* (both morning and evening). There was a healthy competition between the papers for the latest information on the Notre Dame team. Archie Ward, who later found fame is sports editor of the *Chicago Tribune*, was a reporter who covered the Notre Dame team during this time. His account of the 1919 season is perhaps, the best on record.

September 15, 1919

"...With a football schedule that surpasses in caliber of opponents anything ever attempted at Notre Dame staring him in the face, Athletic Director and Head Football Coach Knute Rockne started (practice) this afternoon. It is no ordinary season that gets under way on Cartier Field today."

"Much importance is attached to the new season and it is surprising to note what keen interest is being taken in the Notre Dame team not only by alumni and students of the university, but eastern and western football critics as well. This marks the return of the football game to pre-war standards since the student army training units established in nearly every school is history."

"While the other schools which Notre Dame meets on the gridiron this fall boast of having prospects and plenty of available material to choose from for their teams, Coach Rockne is not in a position to say upon whom he can depend and what the prospects will be until he looks over the candidates."

For the 1919 season, Rockne's backfield teammate Charles "Gus" Dorias, who quarterbacked some great Notre Dame teams in previous years, became assistant coach. His main responsibility was the backfield.

As football practice began, it was clear that a transformation of the program was underway. Players who served in the Army were now available. Professionalism had come to college football. For Notre Dame, the sport became more lucrative. Most of the games were played away from Notre Dame, as other schools put up large purses to lure the team from South Bend.

September 16, 1919

Following the first practice session, there was great concern over the team. Only 40 candidates reported for the first of the two-a-day practice sessions. Many of the players Rockne was counting on were missing. The offensive and defensive lines looked weak.

"Knute Rockne is considerably worried over the prospects of developing a line which can check the advances of the Army (Cadets), the Cornhuskers and the various strong elevens which will oppose the locals this season."

While Rockne struggled with the offensive and defensive lines, it was clear that he had problems in the backfield, though George Gipp was unaccounted for.

"Heading the bevy of backfield performers is Captain Leonard Bahan, a clever player who handles a halfback or quarterback position with equal facility. Besides Bahan there are Brandy, Pearson and Barry, monogram men of 1918, who are prepared to fight for their old berths. In addition, Bergman, Malone, Slackford, Miller and

Fitzpatrick, athletes who fought for Notre Dame before the war are ready to do battle."

September 17, 1919

Frank Coughlin, a big tackle who played for the 1916 varsity team, returned and Rockne was able to feel better about the offensive and defensive line. What brought many of these players back? It is clear that some inducement was provided. Many of the players of this era who returned from the war had difficulty finding jobs. Returning to school to play football was an easy choice, particularly when the school offered incentives to players.

September 18, 1919

Despite the optimism on the campus Rockne was worried about other teams on Notre Dame's schedule.

"...Reports emanating from every camp where Notre Dame opponents bivouac confirm the suspicion that the local athletes have powerful opposition to meet. From Morningside College at Sioux City, comes word that Coach Saunderson is already grooming his men for the mixup with Rockne's Huskies. Similar reports have arrived from Nebraska, the Army, Indiana and Purdue. Combined with reflections on the seemingly weak condition of the Notre Dame line this fall, these reports are not conducive to laughter.

"Within a few days a coterie of students will canvass South Bend in an effort to dispose of several hundred season tickets for the rapidly approaching football season. If they sell like hot cakes and if native fans show indications of supporting a winning eleven, some of the greatest gridiron classics in America will be staged here in 1920. Failure of local people to turn out for contests here in past years is the reason that Notre Dame plays nearly all of its important conflicts on foreign soil. The attendance at the Michigan Aggies and the Western Normal games this fall will be a criterion for Coach Rockne when arranging his 1920 chart."

September 19, 1919
"A drizzling rain restricted morning practice to the gym while the absence of Gipp began to cause concern. offense, to report for duty has aroused a great deal of comment in official circles. Both have signified their intention of returning, but no word has been received from either man in several days."

September 20, 1919
Rockne spent the afternoon briefing his team on football rules and regulations, as optimism returned to the campus. "...Things looked bright on a gloomy afternoon for the Notre Dame football squad when Coach Rockne wheeled his his athletes into the gymnasium after having given them final instruction before the first scrimmage of the season. Although, Rockne's squad is a few days behind the pace set by Purdue, Indiana and the other rivals, he is bringing his men through in fine condition."

September 23-27, 1919
Coach Rockne continued to mold his team into shape during the second week of practice. The first scrimmage, on the 22nd was termed 'miserable.' But, during the next week Dorias and Rockne gradually

formed a battle plan. Pre-war football was concentrated on the ground game. It was called 'old-fashioned football' for a good reason. Many coaches viewed the passing game as too risky or anathema to the traditional game. Dorias brought with him an appreciation of the open, passing game. Notre Dame was forced to concentrate on the open style of football because its line was weak. By September 24th, Notre Dame held its first scrimmage under game conditions.

"...With a quartet of clever backfield men as a common denominator two varsity squads of the Notre Dame football band battled to a scoreless tie on Cartier Field Wednesday afternoon. The scrimmage was fast throughout and was a much better exhibition than the first mix-up of the season staged last Saturday."

"With the approach of the first game of the campaign the enthusiasm of the Gold and Blue campus is growing by leaps and bounds. The number of frenzied fans of the sidelines Wednesday aggregated several hundred. It required the services of a corps of substitute players to prevent the enthusiasts from swarming on the field.

'Dutch' Bergman's scintillating runs were the salient features of Wednesday's scrimmage. He displayed an uncanny precision in picking holes in the line and on several occasions he squirmed and wriggled like human gelatin before pinned to the ground. The work of the linesmen as a whole was mediocre. The performance of Cudahy at tackle, however, saved Pearson's team the ignominy of having their goal desecrated when Bahan's bunch became cantankerous near the case of the scrimmage."

"...Lack of driving power in the interference was the predominating defect of yesterday's exhibition. The athletes showed more aggressiveness and more flashes of a real football team than has been seen on Cartier Field this fall, but the interference must be perfected before success is obtained."

The good news for Notre Dame was the return of George Gipp on the 24th. "...George Gipp, halfback and punter deluxe returned yesterday and was in uniform for afternoon scrimmage. Gipp's belated appearance is attributed to an attack of influenza. He appears to be in good condition and will probably be prepared for heavy work the first of next week."

Gipp had spent much of the summer of 1919 playing baseball for a local Laurium team known as the Aristocrats. Gipp helped his team capture the league title with a 15–1 record by batting .494 with 12 home runs. Fellow teammate Joe Savinni remembered that Gipp was seen as one of the greatest baseball players of his era.

"...Gipp drove the car I was riding in, and we arrived in town about three in the morning. It was quite chilly, and we stopped at a greasy spoon restaurant. As I remember we had to wake up the proprietor to get some hot coffee and a little something to eat. While we were eating I happened to pick up a local newspaper that was on the counter, and on the sports page was this article about our upcoming games. The article mentioned Gipp, saying that we were supposed to have a guy who could field like Tris Speaker (a Hall of Fame outfielder) and hit and run the bases like Ty Cobb. I quickly showed it around to the rest of the guys. I remember George got a big laugh out of it.

After the summer season, Gipp's teammates gave him a leather traveling bag for his trip back to South Bend. On September 21st, the season formally ended with a banquet presided over by Manager Joe Swetish and league president Knauff, then Gipp headed to South Bend, but stopped off in Chicago for a day of gambling.

September 29, 1919
With George Gipp in camp, Notre Dame began its week of practice before the game against Kalamazoo.

"...Local gridiron enthusiasts are anticipating one of the most hectic opening contests ever; staged on Cartier Field when Kalamazoo comes here next Saturday. In 1917 Kalamazoo trounced the Notre Dame freshmen 33–0 and concluded their season with the college championship of Michigan tucked under their blouses. Practically every member of that stellar organization is playing with this year's team and the northerners supporters are hopeful of starting the 1919 season with a victory over Notre Dame."

September 30, 1919
The drive to sell season tickets continued as Gipp and his teammates were finally able to practice together for the first time.

"...The campaign to dispose of several hundred season tickets was opened with a bang last night when four hundred tickets were mailed to South Bend's leading businessmen. The purpose of the drive is to give local fans an opportunity to see the leading football teams of the country perform here. If the fans display sufficient enthusiasm Athletic

Director Rockne promises to bring Nebraska and Purdue to the local field next fall. The following year he will bring Indiana and other strong teams here. But to do this means many more fans must pass through the turnstiles this fall than ever before, as it requires great financial support to card such opposition."

"Nebraska University offers nearly six thousand dollars to get the Notre Dame eleven to their field, and Lincoln, a city no larger than South Bend, turns out the crowd sufficient to warrant such an expense."

It is clear from the newspaper coverage that money was starting to have a big effect on college football at this time. Until George Gipp came to Notre Dame, college football was only a popular gate attraction. Gipp, through his brilliant play, was able to turn-on the South Bend area as no other player had ever done. He became more than a player on the Notre Dame football team. He was Notre Dame, and his rise in prominence meant the decline of academics.

October 1, 1919

Notre Dame continued to prepare for the Kalamazoo game with a hard scrimmage against the freshman team. This, as supporters of Kalamazoo began to feel confident.

"...Supporters of the Kalamazoo tribe are openly predicting victory over the Gold and Blue in Saturday's fray. Reports from the north divulge the information that the Kezooks are powerful and that the Michiganders are prowling around the campus grinning like wolves in anticipation of the result here Saturday."

"The Kalamazoo journalistic ambassador stated that the regulars go through the scrubs like a house on fire and are able to score touchdown after touchdown against them. Coach Young is said to have a wealth of material for a strong backfield. The forward wall looks like a string of boxcars."

October 2, 1919
The varsity team ran "rough-shod" over the freshman team, and "for the first time this season the varsity looked like a championship team."

October 3, 1919
A giant pep rally ended the preparation for the Kalamazoo game. The Notre Dame Blue and Gold were at last ready for their first game.

"The Gold and Blue team is in tip-top condition for the opening of the most promising season in the grid annals of the institution. The lineup in the last practice of the week was Trafton at center, Anderson and Ambrose, guards; Coughlin and Crowley, tackles; Kirk and E. Anderson, ends; Bahan, quarterback; Gipp and Bergman, halfbacks; and Kasper, fullback."

That lineup was to be the main 11 for Notre Dame for the 1919 season. Coach Rockne entered this fall campaign with many question marks in the offensive line and on the day before the first game there was concern whether Notre Dame would be able to handle some of the bigger teams it would face. What wasn't a problem was the ticket drive. At least 5,000 tickets were sold for the first game, as Rockne and Dorias were able to whip up enthusiasm.

Gipp Leads
The Irish to Victory

October 10, 1919

Led by Bergman and Gipp, Notre Dame defeated Kalamazoo 14–0 at Cartier Field. It was a hard fought game that left many Notre Dame fans disappointed. As is the case in many games, the build-up far exceeded the actual event.

The first half featured penalties, mistakes and fumbles. It ended in a 0–0 tie. Both teams were able to move the ball, but every time one neared the others goal a penalty or a turnover got in the way.

Notre Dame was finally able to score in the 3rd quarter. "...Notre Dame came back a different team in the third quarter and immediately assumed the offense. Clever running by Gipp and Malone placed the ball on the 7-yard line. Gipp was injured and replaced by Barry." Bahan was able to sneak the ball over the goal line after Malone barreled down to the two yard line.

"The final score came in the fourth quarter as a result of brilliant individual work by Bergman. He shook off every opponent that touched him, racing 50 yards for a touchdown."

Gipp rushed for 148 yards in 11 carries before leaving the game with a leg injury. It was to be his best rushing effort of the season.

Participants in the game offer conflicting accounts of the contest. According to Charlie Burlingham, the left tackle for Kalamazoo, game officials favored Notre Dame. "Penalties were overlooked regularly when committed by Notre Dame in the late stages of the game," Burlingham said. He claimed that Bergman's 50-yard-run for a touchdown was tainted because of blatant holding by the Notre Dame offensive line.

As for Gipp, Kalamazoo players were effusive in their praise. Forrest "Dutch" Strome said that Gipp "was one of the best backfield men I have ever seen." Defensive left halfback Leslie Mackay said Gipp gave him a difficult game.

"He was indisputably the most effective of the Notre Dame ball carriers," Mackay said. "He took very long, hard-running strides and was hard to bring down. In fact, as far as I was concerned he was impossible to bring down, on a solo tackle. Most of Gipp's runs were to my side, and I spent my full time tackling him and hanging on until someone came along to help. I never brought him down once by myself. We all had great respect for his ability. The first tackler to hit him usually got only one leg for a target."

Miles Casteel, a center for Kalamazoo said Gipp's ability to improvise helped create today's halfback position pass.

"We had Gipp trapped 15 yards behind the line of scrimmage when he ran to his right. As he was running with several of us in hot pursuit, he kept yelling 'Eddie, Eddie, Eddie,' and then he cocked his arm and threw a long pass downfield intended for right end Eddie Anderson, who had gone downfield to block for what started out as an end-run play. This was the first time anyone had ever passed on the run, and I believe it was from this particular play that Rockne soon incorporated the running pass into the Notre Dame box formation."

Other players remembered that Gipp was able to provide the huge crowd with quite a show before the game began.

"When Notre Dame came out on the field, Gipp brought two footballs with him. He stood on the 50-yard line and drop kicked the first one over one goal post, then turned around and proceeded to drop-kick the next one over the other goal post. I remember the crowd let out a tremendous roar of appreciation," said John Thompson, a right end for Kalamazoo.

This show with the two footballs was something that Gipp would repeat many times before games. Joe Mishica was right tackle for Kalamazoo. He was also a friend of Gipp's from his home town. Mishica remembered that Gipp once kicked a ball 100 yards with a strong wind behind him. He grew up with Gipp in Michigan and said Gipp didn't play football because he preferred the poolroom when they were in high school.

"He was a friendly kind, very personable to everyone," Mishica said. "One of the main reasons he never played football for Calumet High was that he preferred playing pool after school rather than going to football practice. He'd head right to the pool hall" right after school.

Mishica, incidentally, knocked Gipp out of a freshman game in 1917 with a clip, which was a legal way of blocking in those days. "I caught George with a clip in the first quarter and he didn't come back until the fourth quarter. Of course, he scored the touchdown that put the game out of reach when he got back in."

"He was a very aggressive player who ran with his knees high. I tackled him head-on a few times and he was one tough runner to bring down."

While Notre Dame won, many of its fans were disappointed by the score. Despite this, the mood was upbeat as Indiana lost and Purdue tied as Notre Dame was beating Kalamazoo. Fans were already looking forward to the game against Indiana on November 1st.

"The Notre Dame-Indiana tilt promises to be the most bitterly contested game in the middle west this fall. The encounter will take place at Indianapolis on November 1st. Both institutions are making plans to transport a goodly portion of their student bodies to the scene of the combat."

Notre Dame
Defeats Mt. Union

Before Notre Dame would face Indiana, it had several important games on its schedule, including a game against Nebraska on October 18th. The next game on the schedule was a contest against Mount Union.

October 8-12, 1919

Notre Dame began practicing for the Mount Union game with an eye toward the game against the Cornhuskers. Many of the players had minor aches and pains from the first game which limited the intensity of the practice.

"...The varsity was deprived of the service of Bahan, Trafton, Degree and Smith, Bergman, Miller, Brandy and Slackford were present for the signal drill, but were unfit for scrimmage and they groped their way back to the showers when hostilities started."

"Unless the condition of the squad improves rapidly before Saturday, it is probable that Coach Rockne will have to pull a bit of super-strategy in one form or another to defeat the fast Mount Union eleven."

On October 9th, Coach Rockne and Dorias began working on a misdirection play with Gipp and Bergman. It was essentially a reverse play on the kick-off. Gipp would take the ball and run to his right with his interference and at the last minute he would hand-off to Bergman, who would run to his left. This play was one of the first uses of reverse-action on the football field. It caused the defense to be suckered-in and with their over-pursuit left a gaping hole for a fast-back. Bergman was the perfect back, since he could do the hundred yard dash in under 10 seconds.

The injuries from the Kalamazoo game left the Notre Dame squad "crippled" and in "mediocre condition." Many observers viewed Mt. Union as a formidable team.

"...The Mount Union men come to Notre Dame with the 1918 Ohio college championship tucked away in their blouses and with a cluster of stars whose power has already been felt in Buckeye circles. The visitors uncorked the season by administering a terrific walloping to Canton and only last Saturday held the powerful West Virginia eleven to a respectable count."

On the day before the game local papers reported that at least five or six players who started the Kalamazoo game would be on the sidelines for the game against Mt. Union and "two or three men who started the game are not expected to last longer than a quarter or a half at the longest."

October 8-12, 1919
George Gipp rushed for 123 yards in 10 carries and passed for 49 yards, as Notre Dame crushed Mt. Union, 60–7. "The Notre Dame men outplayed their opponents in every department of the game. The lop-sided victory

was recorded by the use of simple plays only, a bit of super-strategy on the part of Coaches Rockne and Dorias deployed to deceive visiting scouts who were eager to see Notre Dame in action."

Notre Dame scored nearly four minutes after the opening kickoff as Gipp crashed through on an off-tackle play. Mt. Union quickly tied the score at seven with a long series of perfectly executed pass played. But, that was as close as the team from Ohio would get. Gipp took over the offense, and with a couple of thirty yard runs, went ahead 13–7 at the end of the first quarter. In the second quarter, after the Notre Dame defense held, Gipp threw a 35-yard pass to Kirk, which set up a dash around left end which put Notre Dame up 20–7. After this, Gipp was replaced by Johnny Mohardt, who sprinted 80 yards for a touchdown to make it 27–7. Bergman closed out the scoring with a 25-yard run for a touchdown. Rockne used subs the rest of the way, as Notre Dame piled on the points. The 60–7 win was satisfying for the 4,000 fans at Cartier Field, but not so for Gipp. He didn't like to play in games unless there was a challenge, and the team from Ohio didn't provide much for Gipp.

Mt. Union players said Gipp was unstoppable for the quarter and a half he was in the game. "He was a great broken field runner, and we just couldn't stop him," said end Larry Brown. "He would run to daylight if that were possible, but if he was hemmed in he simply ran over you," said left guard Jim Robinson.

The Journey to Nebraska

Notre Dame began its preparation for the annual game with Nebraska. This series of football contests was perhaps the biggest interstate rivalry for Notre Dame in its early years of football. The game would attract interest from all over the Midwest. All of the battles were memorable.

Notre Dame lost the first game by one point, won the second 20–0, lost the third, 7–0, and was held to a scoreless tie in 1918 as Nebraska played a defensive game with the sole intention of keeping Notre Dame off the scoreboard. They played not to win, but to prevent the Blue and Gold from scoring. Rockne was frustrated by the inability of Notre Dame to score against the Cornhuskers. As practice began, he vowed to find a way to score quickly.

Rockne began tinkering with backfield combinations early in the week. "Coach Rockne is trying every combination imaginable in the backfield in an effort to present a strong scoring machine against the Cornhuskers. Monday he shifted Captain 'Pete' Bahan from quarter to his old position at halfback and Joe Brandy was given command of the team."

Many of the injured players had healed, and as Notre Dame began the trip to Lincoln, the team was in top condition. There was a controversy involving the playing field which surfaced late in the week. In past years, Nebraska's team had outweighed Notre Dame by an average of ten pounds to the man. The Blue and Gold had the faster team, but Nebraska had a "unique" home field advantage. Because of rigid economic conditions, Nebraska had used a dirt field. This sandy, beach-like field was put in during the 1916 season. Notre Dame had yet to score a point on the field and many of its supporters were upset with the way Nebraska ran the show, as a slower field inhibited the fast action of Notre Dame's backs.

Rumor has it that Rockne demanded a different surface for the 1919 game. Nebraska reacted by covering the sandy field with sawdust.

"...The practice sessions of this week are expected to grind the saw dust into top dirt, making the footing better suited to fast football than the ordinary soil. Rains have been persistent this week and the Cornhuskers' management is extremely anxious to put the field in prime shape for the Saturday spectacle.

"In all probability, Nebraska will outweigh Notre Dame," said Head Coach Schulte, "and it might be to our advantage to play the Rockne team on a slow, muddy field, but we are not seeking advantage of that sort. If Notre Dame can out-speed us and hand us a beating, we stand ready to take it without whimpering. The followers of the sport like fast football and that is what we are trying to insure them by covering the field with a layer of sawdust."

This type of field covering was common on football playing surfaces in the Pacific Northwest, where Autumn rains turned many fields into muddy pits. Practically all the schools used sawdust as a way to improve traction.

Nebraska had started the season with a huge defeat by Iowa and a tie against Minnesota. Despite this, the Cornhuskers were viewed as a formidable opponent. Notre Dame took 21 players to Lincoln for the contest on October 18.

October 14-17, 1919

With Bergman leading the way by scoring a touchdown on the first play of the game, Notre Dame defeated Nebraska 14–9 to remain undefeated.

Prior to the game Rockne drilled his team incessantly. As the teams lined up for the opening kickoff, it was time to put the reverse into action. Gipp took the kickoff on the ten-yard line and started running to his right. As the Nebraska coverage team converged on him, he passed a lateral to Bergman, who had clear sailing. Bergman sped down the left sideline, and, after a crunching block by Hunk Anderson ran 90 yards for a touchdown which gave Notre Dame the lead and the advantage it would never lose. In the second quarter the Cornhuskers closed the gap with a touchdown after a long drive. Nebraska missed the extra point and at halftime Notre Dame led, 7–6.

Following intermission, Gipp was again the catalyst for another Notre Dame touchdown. A 44-yard pass to Bergman moved the ball from the Notre Dame 46-yard line down to the Cornhusker ten-yard line. After Notre Dame moved closer on runs by Miller and Bergman, Bahan used a quarterback sneak to get into the end zone. The conversion made it 14–6.

Nebraska closed out the scoring in the fourth quarter with a 40-yard field goal. Notre Dame had finally defeated the team that had been ruining their seasons for the last few years. It was a very satisfying game for Rockne, but not so for Gipp. In 15 carries Gipp gained 70 yards, as Nebraska defenders spent much of the afternoon keying on him. He was able to pass for 117 yards. But, for George Gipp, the final score was unsatisfactory.

Gipp had made a series of bets with gamblers from Lincoln on the night before the game, giving Nebraska ten points. As the game entered the final minutes, Notre Dame got the ball and Rockne began pulling his regular players, bringing in a substitute quarterback. The prudent play was to run the ball, and Rockne instructed his team to keep the ball on the ground and chew up the clock, But, Gipp had other ideas. Since he had money on the game, he wanted to try for another touchdown, although to do this might risk a turnover. Gipp was able to persuade the quarterback to try a few passes. It didn't succeed, and Notre Dame was only able to beat the Cornhuskers by five points.

The First Army Game

The next game on Notre Dame's schedule was against Western Normal of Kalamazoo. This would be the second team from Kalamazoo to face Notre Dame in 1919.

October 23-25, 1919
Rockne and Dorias allowed many of the veteran players to miss practice, as they needed time to recover from the tough Nebraska game. Much of the interest among Notre Dame fans was not in the game against Western Normal, but the game the following week against Indiana.

During those years, being the best football team in the state was an important honor for any squad. There was no trophy or championship, but rather, the notoriety of being recognized by the papers and the fans as the best. Sportswriters couched the contest in terms of a "statewide championship," but it had little to do with a real title.

"...With the approach of the Notre Dame-Indiana game scheduled on November 1st, students and alumni of both institutions are making plans to attend the battle. On the outcome of the conflict will depend the championship of Indiana."

"Defeated by the Gophers last Saturday, the downstate tribe is working hard to get in shape for the big contest. According to reports emanating from Indianapolis the Crimson colors will fly from every nook and corner of the city. They are sparing neither time nor expense in making use of the opportunity to do their bit in winning the state laurels victorious Notre Dame football squad at their headquarters in Lincoln Saturday night. "We want Rockne," the crowd bellowed, after it had halted outside the Lincoln Hotel and Notre Dame players had assembled on the Ninth Street balcony of the hotel and the crowd had sung and cheered itself hoarse, both for Notre Dame and for Nebraska.

"It is always a great pleasure for us to visit Lincoln," said Rockne, "because we are sure of a good game."

As reports of the game revealed, the Nebraska fans received all they want of Rockne and his Gold and Blue "grid" machine. The husker pilot, however, had no alibis to offer for the failure of his heavy aggregation to check the Notre Dame team.

"We were defeated by one of the greatest elevens in the country and one of the cleverest backfields in the history of the game," said Nebraska Coach Schulte.

As for Gipp, Nebraska players remembered him for his passing skill, which netted 117 yards for Notre Dame. "In those days forward passes were not used extensively, and it was difficult to complete passes in that the rules required the passer to be five yards behind the line of scrimmage when passing. A passer was allowed only two incomplete passes in a series of downs. After that there was a five-yard penalty assessed for every incomplete pass, and an incomplete pass in the end zone, regardless of the down, was an automatic touchback. None of these rules seemed to bother Gipp, though. He was a fine passer, and because of his passing, Notre Dame was able to get the touchdown that beat us that day," said Cornhusker fullback Floyd Wright. After a long celebration, Gipp and the rest of the Notre Dame team boarded the train and headed back to South Bend, where fans were preparing more parties.

On the 23rd, a staff correspondent reported that Western Normal was bracing for a big contest with Notre Dame. "Perhaps, never before has the Normal had such a good all-around-team. The return of a number of veterans strengthened by a good freshman class gave William Spaulding, Western State Normal's coach, the best material in years. While the Western State Normal holds out small hope of adding Notre Dame to its string of victories, a low score will be the equivalent, while a tie will be credited a great success."

On the 24th Notre Dame had a light practice and a scrimmage with the freshmen that "enabled the varsity to try out some plays which they expect to pull for the amusement of fans attending the Saturday contest."

There is little mention of Gipp during the middle of the week in either the *The South Bend Tribune* or *The South Bend Times* account of practice sessions. It is clear that Gipp avoided practice at all costs. This trait did not endear him to Rockne, who believed that a player only got better with more practice and drills. But, Gipp was a different kind of player and as the 1919 season went on, it became evident that there was little Rockne could do to get him on the field.

As Gipp would return to the practice field for Thursday and Friday sessions, Rockne would say, "Hello, Gipper, got the asthma today, huh?" Despite the light hearted humor, Rockne felt Gipp's presence on the team was detrimental to keeping discipline. Gipp was able to influence other players, and his forays in the pool hall and nightclubs were viewed as harmful to younger players.

On the 25th, *The South Bend Tribune* reported that the Kalamazoo team was coming into the battle well armed.

"...Encouraged by recent victories over stronger teams, the visitors enter the scrap here confident of victory. They have been preparing for months for this battle and came to Notre Dame in the pink of condition."

"The Kalamazoo school boasts of the best team in its grid annals this fall. When Coach Spaulding assembled his men early in September he found a surplus of experienced performers. Sam Foley, a colored halfback who has been dubbed "the black streak," leads the Wolverines' attack. He is heralded as a terrific plunger and a clever open field runner."

October 26, 1919

Scoring early and often, Notre Dame rolled up a 53–0 victory over Western Normal. "Coach Rockne's men completely manacled the Tutors, scoring two touchdowns in each of the first two quarters, three in the third and one in the final period of play without letting their opponents through for a score and without giving away any formations to Indiana scouts who were present."

"Only twice did the old Gold and Blue break away from straight football. Aided by perfect interference the Catholics broke the Normal line at ease for long gains. Plunges were effective, the Notre Dame backs tore around the ends for long gains and aerial football was successfully worked on various occasions."

"The visitors made only two first downs during the entire play and were unable to break the Catholic line at all times, being on the defensive the majority of the fray. The Normal aggregation, having failed in all their trick formation plays and at straight football" attempted several passes near the end of the game, but "Rockne's men gave a brilliant exhibition at intercepting passes."

Gipp rushed the ball nine times for 85 yards and completed two of three passes for 26 yards, most of this coming in the first half. "Notre Dame opened the scrap in whirlwind fashion scoring. Within one minute and a half after tie referee's whistle opened the play. Slackford was down under Dunlap's boot and ran off ten yards. Malone then tore around left end before perfect interference, throwing off every attempt of the Normal lads to tackle, for 65 yards. Gipp reversed the play carrying the ball around right end for the first touchdown."

Gipp scored another touchdown late in the first quarter, running in from ten yards out after an interception. After this Gipp was pulled from the contest, replaced by Norman Barry. The game turned into a rout in the second quarter, as Notre Dame added two touchdowns. In the second half, Rockne began using second string men in order to save his team for the battle against Indiana. The Subs added three touchdowns in the third quarter and one in the fourth, as the Blue and Gold extended its unbeaten streak.

October 23 to November 1, 1919

This week was marked by nervous anticipation on the Notre Dame campus, as the school readied itself for the game against Indiana. It was the game that everyone in the state was looking forward to. Special trains were set up to transport fans to Indianapolis.

"...The Indiana contest will afford Notre Dame supporters the chance they have been waiting for these many years. The state university is a member of the big ten, the conference which five years ago told Notre Dame that it was not sufficiently strong to mingle with. The Saturday game at Indianapolis will give Notre Dame a chance to prove that it deserved to be ranked among the top teams in the Midwest.

On the 29th, Notre Dame lost the services of Joe Brandy, who was seriously injured. "Brandy's kayo occurred during a grueling scrimmage with the freshmen. The varsity was on defense and Brandy, playing safety, tried to stop the quarterback from crossing the goal line for a marker after he had broken through the first line defense. The varsity field marshall lunged at the runner, the latter's knee striking Brandy just above the right eye causing a deep gash and the loss of much blood. With the assistance of a brace of teammates he groped his way back to the dressing room where his wound received attention."

The injury to Brandy was one that wouldn't happen today. Helmets were used in games, but they were skimpy when compared to today's models. Players who wore the small, donut shaped head-gear were often stigmatized by their teammates for not being tough enough. The football player of this era was tough; he had to be, because the emphasis of the running game made blocking and tackling preeminent. The 'high-tech' passing game was not an element of college football until the ball was redesigned.

On the 30th, Eugene Kessler, a sportswriter for *The South Bend Tribune*, speculated on the importance of the Indiana game. "...By retaining their undefeated record throughout the season, Notre Dame has a chance to become the foremost football team in the country. Although the Gold and Blue eleven will not meet champions of the east and west, they clash with representatives of the east and west which have played title winners. At mid-season form Rockne has one of the strongest squads ever assembled at one school. In the contest against Western Normal, he had men aplenty to substitute at every break in the game and instead of decreasing his team's strength, he increased it."

Kessler went on to write that Bergman, and not Gipp was seen by observers as the star of the 1919 season. "Bergman appears to be the star of the squad. This back has master control of his playing, is a first class open field runner and uses good judgement in carrying out plays."

On September 31, 1919 Notre Dame held its last practice before the trip to Indianapolis. By this time interest in the game had reached fever pitch. "Large delegations of football fans are expected from towns and cities within a radius of 200 miles of Indianapolis. The game has not only attracted a great deal of state interest but middle west interest as well. The Notre

Dame squad, as a whole is in good shape. The loss of Brandy and Malone, crippled members of the squad, will be keenly felt, but with these exceptions the team is in excellent physical condition."

November 2, 1919

On a field ankle deep in mud, Bergman, Gipp and Slackford led Notre Dame to a 16–3 victory that removed all doubt as to who had the best team in the state.

"...The field was in such a condition that Bergman, considered the flashiest backfield man in the west, was unable to hit his stride except in a few instances. He used the 'comeback' play and with it was able to wiggle and squirm through the Indiana team for gains of 10–30 yards."

"After Notre Dame had piled up a 16 point lead early in the third quarter, Coach Rockne removed his entire backfield from the game. It was then that Indiana was able to successfully compete with and halt the attack of the upstaters." The first quarter was scoreless, as the muddy field and the rain curtailed both teams offenses. Late in the second quarter, Hunk Anderson broke through the Indiana line and blocked a punt which was recovered on the five yard line. After two line plunges by Slackford and a run by Gipp failed to gain any ground, Notre Dame got a break. As Gipp was being tackled the ball slipped away and bounced into the end-zone, where Slackford recovered it for a touchdown.

Then, late in the second quarter Notre Dame drove down the field. A 30 yard run by Bergman and some runs by Gipp brought the ball close, and Gipp dropkicked for three points as time was running out in the first half.

"Shortly after the start of the third period, Bergman tore through the Indiana line for a 30 yard run, which placed the ball within the Indiana 30-yard line. Line plunges by Slackford and Gipp carried the ball to the eight-yard line, where Gipp circled his right end for a touchdown." The Gipp touchdown made it 16–0 and clinched another victory.

Indiana kicked a field-goal in the fourth quarter after the Notre Dame defense stopped a drive. The 16–3 win set off a wild celebration in the streets of Indianapolis and South Bend.

"...Saturday night Notre Dame students who remained in South Bend rejoiced with exuberant joy. They lock-stepped over South Bend streets through the hotel lobbies and department stores, taking time to demonstrate their overflowing happiness and appreciation for the remarkable work of their team by giving exhibitions of the snake dance. While this was taking place in South Bend, those students and alumni of the Catholic institution who accompanied the squad to Indianapolis celebrated and hailed their winning warriors as the champion football team of Indiana."

The game with Indiana left Rockne with a series of injuries that gave hope to the Cadets of Army, who were to be Notre Dame's next opponent. "It was not until Sunday morning that Bergman realized that he had been hurt. His knee became so lame that he had to hobble to the station with the aid of a cane. It was discovered that the cartilage had been torn and he was ordered to give the knee complete rest."

"Coach Rockne announced that there is no possibility of Bergman's playing in the big clash at West Point this weekend. Bergman's injury could not have come at a more inopportune time. With the Army game at hand Notre Dame needs all the power it has to uphold the standard of western football in the inter-sectional battle. To add to the discomfiture of Notre Dame fans comes the word that Grover Malone will not be able to replace Bergman. As things stack up at present, George Gipp will have to do the ground gaining for Notre Dame against Army.

The annual clash between Notre Dame and Army was seen by football writers in the east as the most important game of the season. With injuries to some key players, Notre Dame fans were worried about the outcome of the Army game. "Notre Dame football fans have lost tons of pep, and all of their cocksureness which resulted from the easy victory over Indiana. It is the slowly but surely dawning truth that "Dutch" Bergman will not be in trim to lead the Gold and Blue attack." Bergman had gained 84 of the 161 total yards that Notre Dame gained in the game against the Hoosiers. His absence made Army the favorite.

November 8, 1919

The South Bend Tribune reported that most of the gamblers were putting their money on Army. "Few contests attract more general attention than the mix between the Cadets and Notre Dame. In all-around importance it ranks with the Harvard-Yale clash. Everything points to a bitterly contested struggle this afternoon. In some spots where Army dough, predominates, the Cadets are on the upper end of 10–9 odds."

Map showing the location of Calumet, Michigan on the Kewanee Peninsula where George Gipp was raised.

Gipp's home in Laurium, a small village next to Calumet.

View of downtown Calumet, Michigan.

Michigan House in Calumet, Michigan where George Gipp and Angelo Stappas waited tables and played cards with the miners.

Calumet High School where Gipp attended classes.

Above: Gekas Candy Kitchen in Calumet, Michigan where Gipp learned how to become a waiter, a skill which enabled him to work part time while at Notre Dame.

Below: Oliver Hotel in South Bend, Indiana where Gipp's team achieved victory in South Bend's first three-cushion billiards championship.

Above: Calumet-Laurium baseball champions, 1919. Gipp is far right, middle row, manager Joe Swetish is next to him.
Below: Notre Dame's 1919 undefeated champions, Gipp is third from left in top row. To his immediate left is Hunk Anderson and Knute Rockne is far left in middle row.

Left, Ronald Reagan portraying George Gipp in the film *Knute Rockne-All American.* Right, George Gipp.

Three of George Gipp's close friends. Top, Angelo Stappas; bottom left, Joe Mishica (coached baseball at Calumet High School & played opposite Gipp with Kalamazoo); bottom right, girlfriend from Laurium, who was Gipp's last date, Northwestern game, 1920.

Top, Gipp looks on at 1st quarter action against Valparaiso, the game where Rockne started his second unit, an unheard of action.

Bottom, men who make up three all-American elevens selected by Walter Camp.

19 20

CAMP'S ALL-AMERICA

GIPP · F. B.

STINCHCOMB H.B.

WAY H.B.

CARNEY · E.

LOURIE · Q.

FINCHER · E

KECK · T

CALLAHAN · G

STEIN · C

WOODS · G

SCOTT · T

Top, George Gipp's grave in Laurium, Michigan.

Bottom, The George Gipp monument in Laurium.

But, while two backfield men were out of the Army game, Notre Dame still had its offensive line intact. For Gipp, the Army game gave him an opportunity for more gambling. He was able to place $100 on the Army game.

A more interesting story about the Army game involved General Douglas MacArthur, who related a story about the game after World War II to Harry Hogan, an illustrious Notre Dame alumnus.

MacArthur's story revealed that Army may have had some of Notre Dame's plays before the game. When the General ran into Hogan he told the story about the play-book.

"We sent a scout out before the Army-Notre Dame game one year and for one reason or another he failed to see the game," MacArthur told Hogan. "But the fellow had nerve enough to explain his plight to Rockne, hoping the great coach would intercede without coach, Mr. Daly."

"Rockne was magnanimous about it. Not only did he feel sorry for our scout, but he provided him with complete diagrams of the Notre Dame plays."

"When our scout came back and told the complete story of how he happened to miss seeing Notre Dame in person, we decided not to make use of the information Rockne so generously provided. If he was cavalier (and Hogan here quoted the General exactly) enough to help us, we decided not to take undue advantage of the information."

"Nonetheless, we were a good team and pretty well prepared for George Gipp. So there we were. Rockne tried to be big-hearted and give us the plays. We decided not to make use of the information, but one of his players gave it to us on the field. As we couldn't do a thing to stop him (Gipp)."

November 10, 1919

In a hard fought game, Notre Dame defeated Army 12–9, as Gipp and Bahan made extensive use of the forward pass. Gipp ran the ball 15 times for 70 yards and passed for another 115 yards on seven completions in 14 attempts. His ability to pass made all the difference, as Notre Dame fell behind 9 to 0 in the first quarter.

In the second period, Notre Dame began making gains which brought the team close to the goal line. Time was running out on Notre Dame. In an article on Gipp by Rev. John O'Brien, called *Notre Dame's 12th Player*, the author tells how Gipp's quick thinking allowed Notre Dame to score.

"...The Cadets had a slight lead. But Notre Dame came back with a passing attack that culminated with a bullet-like shot from Gipp to Bahan on Army's one-yard line. The teams had lined up and Larson, at center, was waiting for the quarterback to start calling signals. Suddenly Gipp called sharply:"

"Pass me the ball!"

"Catching it while the players of both teams stood frozen in their tracks, he dived over for a touchdown. It was none too soon. For just as the ball touched Gipp's fingers, the official sounded the horn for the end of the half. Out of the corner of his eye, Gipp had caught a momentary glimpse of the official beginning to raise the horn to his lips. He realized only a second or two remained."

Rockne was to say later that he never saw such a quick piece of thinking. But, as the team left for half-time Rockne was upset with Gipp. For throughout most of the first half Gipp had improvised on the field.

"George, I'm really sorry my offense isn't good enough for you," Rockne said sarcastically. "It's too bad you had to go through all that trouble of making up plays on the field."

Gipp just smiled. "Now coach," he said, "don't get yourself excited. I've got a hundred bucks bet on this game and we've got to win it."

Rockne was furious, but he let Gipp start the second half. In the fourth quarter, with Notre Dame behind, 9–6, Gipp passed to Bahan, who ran the ball down to the Army four-yard line. On the next play, back-up fullback Walter Miller smashed over right tackle for the touchdown that gave Notre Dame the victory.

The South Bend Tribune article on the Army game praised the effort by Army and the work of Gipp. "Standing head and shoulders above every individual player on the field was George Gipp of Notre Dame. His clever forward passing turned the tide against the Army. His end runs and stellar defensive work assisted materially in the victory."

"Never did a football team fight harder than the sons of West Point on the wind sprayed plains of New York on Saturday, never did an Army eleven show more courage in the face of odds. But all the fight and courage which the Cadets could develop was not sufficient to stop the equally courageous and more powerful team which carried the colors of Notre Dame."

The win over Army touched off another wild celebration in South Bend. "Banners, proclaiming the Notre Dame team as *The Champions of the West,* were carried through the streets. Others carrying the motto *Notre Dame Always Wins* were carried. Saturday night the student body paraded down the uptown streets, carrying banners and making noise, to satisfy their overjoyed satisfaction of the showing against Army."

Notre Dame still faced three more games. The next opponent, Michigan State had given Rockne the only defeat of his career up until that point. The Michigan Aggies were always able to get up for games against Notre Dame. The South Bend papers hyped up the game against the Aggies.

"...Undergraduates at the Michigan institution are stepping briskly around the campus, each with a well sized chip on his shoulder, ready to battle if any Notre Dame adherent can be found. The Aggies can be clawless against any team but Notre Dame. Against this old enemy the northerners are expected to knuckle down to their best labors, to supply every ounce of strength needed in every action and to fight to the last breath. Men who make the Aggie team in the Notre Dame game do so through a season of hard work and they go into this supreme contest filled with a desire to achieve fame. The Michigan lads are keyed to the minute and will make their class felt before the game is over."

As the week began, many were still reliving the game against Army. "The work of Gipp and Bahan in the big inter-sectional struggle undoubtedly won them consideration as material for the all-American eleven. Gipp was a veritable catapult hurling the oval to any and all sections of the field with such bullet like speed and accuracy that the soldiers threw their arms in disarray. New York newspaper representatives declared that the overhead attack of the Notre Dame eleven was the greatest exhibition of open work ever seen in the east. It even surpassed the famous attack of Notre Dame in 1913 in which Rockne and Dorias, then proteges of Jesse Harper, helped to administer the worst drubbing the Army ever suffered. The attack was cleverly conceived and brilliantly executed. Gipp's hurling was largely responsible for the success of the venture."

What made football such a popular sport at Notre Dame? Why did it receive the interest? Part of the secret behind the success of the program at Notre Dame was revealed in a behind the scenes article in *The South Bend Tribune* on November 12th. It showed how the school had become a "football factory".

"...Football receives no little amount of attention at Notre Dame. Everyone at the school has an opportunity to take part in the great college sport and learn the fundamentals of the game. This is due to the winning aggregation turned out by the university year after year."

"A great inter-hall system of competition, which is now in progress, furnishes abundant material for all forms of athletics. Nowhere has the idea been so highly developed as at Notre Dame. In football, for instance, the different halls are each represented with an eleven. In certain halls there are two teams, the heavies and the lightweights. A schedule is opened early in October which provides intramural exhibitions for the entire season. The series is conducted under supervision of the board of athletic control. Coaches Rockne and

Dorias have no part in the campaign with the possible exception of arranging the charts."

"The teams practice on free days and are tutored by some student who has a working knowledge of the game. Occasionally a varsity player undertakes to teach the youngsters the rudiments of the game during his free hours. All students, except candidates for the varsity eleven, are eligible for the series. Consequently, many hectic combats ensue."

"...Many athletes of calibre are uncovered in these contests who otherwise might never be known. Year after year the varsity is built up on the products of the inter-hall series. With very few exceptions the members of the 1919 eleven, heralded as the fastest team in the west, is composed entirely of former hall stars."

"Similar series are held in basketball, baseball and track. In this way athletics are kept up to a certain standard year after year, a feat productive of unbounded envy from other institutions."

"There is a reason why athletics should include a part of the education received by young men of the country. Universal training, which is being advocated by statesmen at this time, is nothing more than compelling men to take a certain amount of exercise and drills in which commands are readily obeyed. An editorial in a leading American magazine, during the war contained the comment: 'If every American soldier learns to play football, our country would have the greatest Army in the world. Athletics have the same effect upon the student as does military training.'"

"General Pershing was quoted as saying before the war ended that an Army organization was like a football team in which every man is trained to physical perfection under strict discipline, but is capable of brilliant individual action in a crisis. He added, 'We want our men trained in the same way.'"

"Surely the war was a great vindication of athletics and football in particular. There is no question that as a class the athletes made the best soldiers. They are physically fit and had the best equipment for meeting emergencies and handling themselves in the pinches."

"Football aims to coordinate the mental and physical activities under the spur of command signals, which are generally similar to those of preparatory and execution commands used in military work. It creates and develops the habit of constantly and unfalteringly obeying the initiative given by a command when the person trained is in immediate contact with the maximum of opposition, whether the same be offensive or defensive, and in this way fortifies and habituates the mind to obeying orders at the moment when direct results may occur."

"More than any other form of physical training, football compels the player to realize his individual capacity as a part somewhere in its treatment of fundamentals does not hold up football as the proper conception for men who wish to appreciate properly the work of individual as part of the mass."

The week of November 12th through the 15th marked the 50th anniversary of the first college football game, between Princeton and Rutgers.

"The game has undergone great changes since the first contest was played. It is now a game where science and wit counts, while in the first scrap physical strength was the predominating factor for the victor. For this reason, perhaps, 1919 has seen the most thrilling games of any previous season's play, in which agonizing suspense, dashed hopes, close scores and action have been the outstanding characteristics." The passing game was perhaps the single element that differentiated the game of the 19th century from the game of 1919. It allowed smaller players to compete and opened the field for more offensive displays. This brought more fans in, while increasing the importance of college football to schools all over the country.

November 15, 1919

Gipp arrived back in South Bend after a mysterious absence. He had disappeared shortly after the game with Army. Coach Rockne decided to punish Gipp by starting the second string players. "Cy Degree, tackle, will be the only regular player to start the contest. If possible, Rockne will trounce the Aggies with a second string lineup, thus saving his regulars for the grueling tilt with Purdue."

November 16, 1919

In a game featuring the Notre Dame aerial game, the Blue and Gold defeated the Michigan Aggies 13–0 in the final contest of the year.

Sportswriter Eugene Kessler wrote that Notre Dame played it safe and close to the vest. "...Notre Dame football players had an off-day at the game Saturday, partly due to over-confidence but mostly because Coach

Rockne wanted to save his team for the Purdue scrap
next weekend."

"With this end in view, Coach Rockne opened the
Aggie fray with the second string men. After these men
had held their own against the offense offered by the
visitors, he sent in his first string of gridders, but it was
evident that the famous aggregation which whipped the
Army were playing a safe game. They took no chances
and when the opposing line offered a defense, with the
determination to hold the Gold and Blue rushes at any
cost, they were permitted to carry out their desires
without extra exertions on the part of the Catholic scoring machine. Degree's punting saved the Notre Dame
line from being compelled to put forth extra efforts in
keeping the visitors from crossing the Irish goal."

After a scoreless first quarter, Gipp and other first
string players were sent into the game. Early in the
quarter the Aggies tried a fourth down; pass from their
own 35-yard line. Gipp batted it down, and Notre
Dame took over. Gipp completed a 20 yard pass to Kirk
which gave Notre Dame a great scoring chance. Two
carries by Slackford and one by Gipp gave Notre Dame
a first and goal from the three-yard line. But, Gipp
fumbled a handoff and eventually recovered the ball on
the Aggie eight-yard line. On fourth down a pass play
failed and the Aggies were able to take over. But, their
bad field position put them at a disadvantage and they
were forced to punt.

On their next possession, Notre Dame started from
the Aggie 38-yard line. After runs by Slackford and
Bahan gave Notre Dame a first down, Gipp was on the
receiving end of a five yard pass. Another Gipp pass to

Kirk gained twelve yards. Bahan smashed through the Aggie line for ten yards and Slackford scored the first touchdown on an off-tackle play. Notre Dame maintained its 6–0 lead until the fourth quarter when Notre Dame was able to capitalize on a bad Aggie punt. Starting from Michigan's 35-yard line, Notre Dame was able to score another touchdown as Gipp passed to Coughlin on a tackle eligible play. The game ended with a 13–0 victory for Notre Dame. Gipp ran for 45 yards in ten carries and completed five of ten passes for another 73 yards in the victory.

John Hammes, a star fullback for the Aggies said Gipp's short passes to Kirk gave Notre Dame the win. "I saw many a short pass thrown by Gipp that I couldn't get my hands on. And several times in the game I had a good chance to tackle him, but because of his shifty running, missed him completely."

October 18, 1919

The Purdue game was beginning to attract a great deal of interest. Many observers felt that the game would provide a good barometer of the ability of Notre Dame's team. Ohio State was viewed as the top team in the midwest but the Buckeyes lost a game to Illinois. The Ohio team played Purdue and was only able to beat them by a touchdown. The Boilermakers were the only common opponent for Notre Dame and football experts were looking to compare Notre Dame and Ohio State by seeing how well each did against Purdue. If Notre Dame would be able to beat Purdue by more than a touchdown, then it could be ranked among the top teams in the region. Sportswriters began hyping the contest to a fever pitch.

"...By the showing of the individuals in the Notre Dame-Purdue game may depend chances for all-western berths. The record of gridiron hostilities between these universities, rivals almost from the inception of the game, glows with the glory of the heroes who soared to greatest sportive heights for the honor of their alma mater."

"The South Bend eleven is in great shape for the impending battle and for the first time since the Indiana game the locals will throw their full strength against an opponent. The recovery of Bergman, halfback, enables Rockne to start the strongest lineup at his command. The team came through its victory over the Aggies without waste of man power."

Both Purdue and Notre Dame will carry into the arena a full quota of stars, well mated henchmen who have already established themselves among the foremost players of the day. The Lafayette crew will have Huffine, Wagner and Meeker upon whom the downstate fans are banking their hopes of victory over their ancient foe."

"Notre Dame, too, boasts of some of the greatest individual players in its grid annals. It is hard to find a more fleet and elusive open field runner than Bergman and a more accurate hurler of the forward pass than Gipp."

November 19-21, 1919

Both teams began preparations for the big contest. At Purdue, Coach Scanlon spent hours rehearsing Notre Dame's offensive plays. "...Coach Scanlon has been pointing his men for the Notre Dame game for several weeks and his athletes are prepared to add a final staggering upset to a season replete with reverses by grabbing the state title Saturday."

"Purdue and Notre Dame clashed in the final game of the season at Lafayette last year and the Gold and Blue emerged from the combat on the proper side of the score. The downstate clan is determined to make up for that defeat when it opposes Bahan's bunch this season. The supporters of the Boilermakers are predicting a close, hard-fought battle. If the manner in which Scanlon's men are smothering Notre Dame's plays in daily scrimmage with the freshmen is a criterion, something unexpected may happen this weekend. The Purdue regulars find little or no difficulty in smearing their overhead attacks. However, smothering an attack of the Purdue freshmen is an altogether different proposition from breaking down Notre Dame's varsity drive."

November 23, 1919

Before a huge crowd of 7,000, Notre Dame defeated Purdue 33–13.

Gipp was the main star for Notre Dame, completing 11 of 15 passes for 217 yards and rushing for 51 yards on 12 carries. "It was a glorious thing for Notre Dame that George Gipp was in the lineup. Uncovering a brilliant and amazing assortment of overhead passes that whizzed through the air like black streaks, the big Notre Dame halfback thrilled players and spectators alike. To Kirk, Bergman and Coughlin can Rockne's men give credit for the fact that Notre Dame passed its way to 217 yards via the aerial route. To one of these three men Gipp hurled the ball with uncanny accuracy and it was not his fault that more passes were not completed."

For most of the first quarter Purdue controlled the ball. But, they were unable to get points on the board. In the second quarter Notre Dame opened up its passing attack.

Bergman scored on an end run of twelve yards after passes by Gipp had brought the ball downfield. Late in the second quarter, Gipp connected with Kirk for another touchdown as Notre Dame built up a 13–0 half-time lead.

The second half was all Notre Dame, and the final score of 33–13 left the Blue and Gold as the only undefeated team in the Midwest.

On the day after the Purdue game, Gipp, Bergman, Madigan and other Notre Dame players sneaked over to Rockford, Illinois, to play professional football. The game had been arranged by Slip Madigan, who learned that some Purdue players had been hired to play for one of the Rockford teams. The local newspapers didn't reveal the names of any of the players who participated in the contest. Gipp and his cohorts were paid $150 a piece for the game, which was won by the team using Notre Dame's players. If any of the players had been caught it would have meant immediate loss of eligibility.

It is clear that Rockne knew about the contest, but did nothing to stop it. In the game Bergman injured his leg. This limited his participation in the game against Morningside on Thanksgiving Day.

November 25, 1919

The South Bend Tribune reported that Bergman and Madigan had injuries. This was not reported in the papers account of the Purdue game. The only conclusion that can be reached is that the two injured themselves in the professional pickup game. The paper however, maintained that the injuries occurred during the Purdue game.

The locals, however, were not overconfident on the eve of their departure. The Iowa eleven is known to have a terrific drive in its attack and it has a defense that at times appears impenetrable. But the westerners will be unable to cope with Notre Dame's baffling overhead attack is the consensus of opinion in this section of the country."

" 'Slip' Madigan, stellar pivot man, played his last game in a Gold and Blue moleskin last Saturday. Early in the game he received a thump over the eye which bursted a small blood vessel, necessitating his retirement from the game for the balance of the season. Trafton will start the game in Madigan's place and Meagher will act as first substitute."

"Bergman was nursing a sore knee and Slackford an injured ankle when the Notre Dame party shoved off from the Lake Shore station today, but both backfield stars are expected to be in shape to play part of the game."

November 26, 1919

As Notre Dame prepared for the final game of the season, sportswriter Arch Ward wrote that the team's use of the forward pass during the 1919 season had caused a fundamental change in the direction of football. "Coach Rockne has taught the football world the advantages of the forward pass with his Notre Dame eleven this fall. Never in the history of the game was this style of play used to better advantage than by the Gold and Blue this fall. It was the last means of attack and it never' failed to come through. Against the Army, against Indiana and against Nebraska and Purdue it was the overhead attack that spelled defeat and dismay for the locals opponents."

"Three factors have been prominent in Notre Dame success with the forward pass. First of all, it has a pair of clever instructors who where proficient in this style of play when they were university players. They worked long and hard to devise an attack that would baffle the foe and their teams success testifies for their abilities. Secondly, the Gold and Blue tribe possesses the most expert passer in the country in George Gipp. He hurls the ball with speed and accuracy to any and all parts of the field."

November 27, 1919
Notre Dame closed its season with a 14–6 win over Morningside College in Sioux City, Iowa.

The game was played in a driving snowstorm with ten degree temperatures. Gipp was the outstanding player on the field, gaining four yards in 14 carries and passing for 66 yards with six completions in eleven attempts.

Notre Dame had to come from behind as Morningside scored after ten minutes of play to grab a 6–0 lead. Gipp's passes set up the go-ahead touchdown in the second quarter, as Bergman plunged through the line. In the third quarter a long pass from Gipp to Kirk gave Notre Dame its final score.

Midway through the third quarter Gipp, thoroughly disgusted with the snow and the ice, went over to the sidelines and stood in front of Rockne.

"I'm through for the day," said Gipp.

"Like hell you are," Rockne answered.

Eventually Gipp left the field and ended his 1919 season. For Notre Dame, the season had been arguably its greatest to date. A record of 9 wins and no losses gave the team recognition as the best in the Midwest.

For Gipp, the season brought him into national prominence. Sportswriters from the East who had seen his performance against Army wrote that he was the best player in the country. He ran for 729 yards in 106 attempts for an average gain of nearly seven yards per carry. His passing, 41 of 72 for 727 yards, made him the pre-eminent player on Notre Dame's team.

December 2-5, 1919

Following the game at Morningside, Coach Rockne attempted to set up a game with Oregon, an undefeated team from the West Coast. Oregon had proposed a game on Christmas Day, in order to decide once and for all, just which team had the best group in the country. The proposed game ran into trouble with teachers at Notre Dame, who felt that too much time had already been spent on football.

"...Storms of protest greeted the invitation tempered the proteges of Rockne and Dorias to appear in the far west. The faculty at Notre Dame, just as at many other universities, is opposed to post season contests. Convinced of the educational value of the trip, however, and due to the fact that no time will be lost from class work, the authorities granted Coach Rockne permission to lead his eleven over the Rockies."

"In naming Notre Dame as the opponent for the western eleven in the holiday attraction, the Oregon school is confident that it picked the strongest team in the country. Officials considered the matter carefully before extending the invitation. Princeton, Harvard, Illinois and other teams were rumored to have been the lucky aggregation, but the western authorities waited patiently to compare the eastern and western elevens. After Notre Dame ran up more points on Purdue than any eleven to oppose it, the Gold and Blue tribe was immediately selected."

On December 3rd, Arch Ward wrote that Rockne was most responsible for the success of the football program of the 1919 season. "Much credit for the success of the Notre Dame eleven must be attributed to Knute Rockne, head coach, athletic director and chemistry instructor at the university. Liked by everyone with whom he comes in contact, Rockne has won a host of admirers for Notre Dame this fall. He is a strict disciplinarian but a man with a heart and one of consideration. He never asks a pupil on the gridiron to do what he would not do himself."

"Followers of the Gold and Blue are mindful of the fact that Rockne has a strategic assistant in 'Gus' Dorias, all-American quarterback of 1913. That Notre Dame had one of the most powerful backfields in the country is due in no small degree to the work of Dorias, who devoted most of his time in perfecting the attack."

December 5, 1919
The proposed game against the Oregon Aggies was cancelled as players started to drift away. Arch Ward summed up the season with an article praising Rockne and Dorias.

"Rockne taught his men a mystifying sort of an attack that overcame physical handicaps and earned the locals the title of the most formidable aggregation in the west. Notre Dame learned much about football that it never expected to know, and that Indiana, Purdue, Ohio State and other western teams have yet to learn."

"There never has been any doubt as to Rockne's ability as a coach, but it took the slashing victories over Nebraska, Army, Indiana and Purdue to establish him as one of the leading chieftains of the day."

For George Gipp, the end of football meant a return to the classroom. On December 14th members of the Notre Dame football team celebrated the championship season at the Oliver Hotel. "In a gala affair arranged by Rockne and Dorias, which featured plenty of food, jokes, soloists and songs and otherwise catchy strains from a university orchestra, George Hull gave a talk as a loyal rooter of the Irish amid a bombardment of cheers."

After monogram letters were awarded, the team held the election for team captain for the 1920 season. In what must be considered the highlight of his career at Notre Dame, Gipp edged out Frank Coughlin by a single vote. His election as captain was a goal that Gipp had waited a long time to achieve, but as time went on, his position was temporary.

After his election, Gipp began to celebrate. On the next night Gipp entered a billiards contest.

"The city billiards contest held at Hull and Calnon's is in the last lap. The tournament will close the latter part of this week. In matches Saturday night, Gipp defeated Vermande, and Beistle won from Baumbach.

Both winners made a high run of three during the games."

Gipp eventually lost the billiards match in the final round. He recovered to win the championship, however, and was named the champion pool player of South Bend on January 10th.

When he wasn't playing pool, Gipp would have all-night poker parties at the Oliver Hotel and Hullie and Mike's. His luck wasn't that good with the cards. These activities eventually caused some embarrassment to school officials at Notre Dame. It was one thing for football players to celebrate and have fun, but it was quite another for the captain of the football team to drink, gamble and enjoy nightlife.

The late night parties left Coach Rockne embarrassed. Much of the consternation was directed at Father John Cavanaugh, who had been instrumental in creating the climate for athletics at Notre Dame. Father Cavanaugh enjoyed the success of the Notre Dame football team. The heightened publicity and the recognition that the team gave the small school helped to turn the school around. As the team became more successful, more money started coming in. The football team came to dominate life on campus.

What also was apparent during this time was the increased influence that Rockne began to have on the campus. This was all derived from the success of the football team. But, as the 1919 season ended, a different era was sweeping America. The campaign for prohibition picked up steam, as more and more states began to approve a Constitutional Amendment which would ban the sale of liquor.

Public morality became a big issue in the United States, and particularly in Indiana. The long bastion of conservative Republicanism, the Temperance Movement found a willing audience in South Bend. The social setting of the time made George Gipp a natural enemy to those who sought to clean-up Notre Dame.

As Gipp became enraptured in all-night parties, he began to neglect his classwork. He began sleeping late in order to catch up on sleep he missed, and then began cutting classes with increasing regularity. Professors at the school were extremely concerned about his class attendance. One professor said, "With a little application he could easily have been a *summa cum laude* graduate and I feel he would have made a superb attorney."

Hunk Anderson wrote that around this time Coach Rockne told him, "George could be the smartest lawyer in the United States if he would settle down to the books."

But, Gipp was having too much fun, both with gambling and with women around South Bend. In December Gipp began keeping steady company with a woman named Iris. Her father was a prominent Indianapolis attorney. He didn't have much use for football players in general and George in particular. Iris was told not to see Gipp anymore. That only brought the two closer. The couple took great pains to make sure that their dates were kept a secret. George began taking the train to Indianapolis five nights a week.

Very few of Gipp's friends knew anything about the relationship. What was known was that Gipp became quite enamored and spent a great deal of time with her at the Bamboo Inn, a Chinese restaurant next door to the Circle Theater. Iris was a petite brunette who lived near 25th and Central in Indianapolis.

But, from the start, the relationship was doomed. Gipp's interest in gambling, night life and pool shooting rubbed Iris the wrong way. Eventually the two split up.

On March 2nd, Gipp decided to try his hand at baseball again. Gus Dorias was now the manager and Gipp felt he would be able to have a better time at baseball with him as manager. But, Dorias was nervous about having a player like Gipp on the team. While he was greatly impressed with his talent, he was also worried about the effect Gipp would have on the younger players. In addition, school officials were getting more and more concerned with Gipp's activities. Father Cavanaugh was transferred to Washington, D.C. and replaced by Father James A. Burns, a hard, tough school administrator.

After a few days of practice, baseball scouts came over from Chicago to watch Gipp play. When he found out that scouts were watching him, Gipp approached Hunk Anderson, who was a catcher for the Notre Dame team.

"How about giving me a hint of what's going to be thrown by the pitcher when I'm in the batter's box today?" Gipp asked.

"Okay," Hunk replied.

After Gipp stepped into the batters box, Anderson asked the pitcher to throw one fastball after another. Gipp proceeded to belt every pitch thrown either off the wall or out of the ballpark. Hunk Anderson later recalled, "The scouts were really impressed with

George, and both of them handed him a contract. Both contracts were identical, calling for a salary of $4,000 a year."

Gipp later turned over the contracts to Anderson for safe keeping. If he had signed one of the contracts, it is quite likely that Gipp would have enjoyed a long baseball career. His ability in baseball probably was greater than football. On the day he got the contract, Gipp went out celebrating. He wound up at Michigan Street's Tokyo Dance Hall, a nightspot that had a well-earned reputation as a "den of iniquity." Gipp was spotted by a faculty member, who reported his presence at the nightspot to Father Burns. On March 8th, Gipp was called into the office and told that he was expelled from school. Later Coach Rockne would claim that Gipp's expulsion didn't result from being seen at an "off-limits" nightclub.

"Gipp was kicked out for missing too many classes. It seemed too late to do anything except scold him, and that was profitless. Yet when I talked to him on his remissness and told him that he had put the finish to a brilliant athletic career, he quietly asked me why he couldn't have an oral examination. Townsmen of South Bend even appealed to the school authorities to give Gipp another chance."

The pressure exerted on Father Burns was quite substantial. Gipp had many supporters among businessmen in South Bend. His patronage of restaurants and hotels was greatly appreciated. Where Gipp went action followed. Notre Dame football had by then, become a tourist attraction. *The South Bend Tribune* and the morning newspaper, *The Herald*, assigned reporters to follow the case. While they covered other sports at Notre Dame, it was football that dominated, both in length and quantity of articles.

Gipp's expulsion was quite a blow to the business establishment. For them, it was a loss of a meal ticket. For the newspapers, there was the possibility that Notre Dame's football team would not be quite as formidable. For Coach Rockne, it was a substantial blow. Bahan had already used up his eligibility, and Rockne didn't have anyone who could throw the ball like Gipp. In later years, Rockne would say that Gipp was treated the same way his other players were treated. He said he arranged an oral examination for Gipp.

The story went that Gipp went into a room with a few professors and answered questions and passed. This account is not entirely accurate. Rockne did lobby for his reinstatement, but he did not arrange an oral examination. That would have been quite extraordinary, as it was against school policy to treat athletes as special cases.

Fr. Burns was inundated with calls from citizens throughout the area, urging him to reinstate Gipp and warning him that his great football player might be lost to another school. During this time college athletics was governed by few controls. The use of professional type players was well documented. There was a whole group of athletes that showed up at the training field at the beginning of baseball or football season. Many were not students, but migrant workers who toiled professionally for one college or another. Without rules to cover participation, schools were free to recruit athletes playing for other schools.

If a school saw that an athlete was unhappy with either the coaching or academic requirements there was nothing to stop them from trying to lure athletes away. Many of the most bitter football rivalries have their origins because of these incidents. Gipp moved all of his belongings to the Oliver Hotel after he was expelled. Nearly a month after he was expelled, Gipp showed up on the campus again, as an umpire in an exhibition game with a team from Mishawaka. While he waited around South Bend, working as a house player at Hullie and Mike's, the University of Michigan offered him a scholarship.

This was followed by offers from "Pop" Warner at the University of Pittsburgh and from Douglas MacArthur at West Point. During all this time, pressure increased on Father Burns. There was letter writing, petitions and public appeals. Finally on April 29th, Father Burns gave in and reinstated Gipp.

Little is known of Gipp's activity at this time, as a conflicting account has emerged over the incident surrounding Gipp's expulsion and reinstatement. On March 9, 1920 *The South Bend Tribune* reported on spring football practice. In this article, *Rockne Begins Spring Drill for Grid Squad,* reporter Arch Ward paints a different picture of the incident.

"...Spring football work at Notre Dame began at noon today with a lecture by head Coach Knute Rockne. The grid talks will take place every day through the preliminary training. The day of the dawdler is over. Within a few days the Gold and Blue squad, with a lineup of rookies blended with veterans, will get in action on Cartier Field. From now on it will be action to the fullest. Rockne has started with a bound and he intends to drive his gridders harder than ever this spring."

"Frank Coughlin, giant tackle of the 1919 eleven, was elected captain of the 1920 team at a meeting of the monogram men yesterday evening. The election followed the withdrawal of George Gipp, captain-elect, from the university. The loss of Gipp is the second big jolt given next autumn's outlook. The disbarment of Trafton two months ago was the first bit of spice sprinkled on the winter dope. Gipp was unanimously selected for an all-western halfback last fall and he was expected to be the mainspring in the Notre Dame's puzzling style of open play next season."

"Notre Dame players are to be commended on the selection of Frank Coughlin as leader of the football team. Discounting what the future will bring for him, Frank's stellar performance to date top his name with former athletic idols of the Gold and Blue." There were reports that Gipp was upset at Coughlin, allegedly telling a close friend, "I wouldn't take it if he offered it — but he should have offered it."

Gipp later told others that his one great disappointment at Notre Dame was that he was never able to make captain. It was probably a minor frustration, at best. Gipp was captain for a period of four months and had he paid more attention to his studies and to student life he would have been captain for the 1920 season. Where does the truth lie in this controversy? One account has Gipp being expelled for his class work and being reinstated after a special examination. Another account has Father Burns caving in to the pressure of fans and alumni and reinstating Gipp in order to prevent him from playing for another football team in the fall. The newspaper account reports that Gipp had "withdrawn" himself from Notre Dame.

The newspaper account is probably to most credible. Other schools were actively courting Gipp and it is clear from Gipp's actions that he had grown tired of Notre Dame.

A week after spring practice began, the football rules committee changed some of the regulations. Many of these new rules were designed to open-up the game. "Football will be played next fall without the punt-out after a touchdown, forward passes will be employed more often because of the new protection given to the thrower, and rough tactics will be lessened because of aided penalties. Other changes proposed by coaches were rejected. Such proposals as compulsory numbering of players, decreasing the span of goal posts, measuring periods by 40 plays instead of 15 minutes, an awarding of points for rushes to within the 25-yard line or after five first downs in succession were investigated thoroughly but discarded."

These new proposals were to make college football more exciting. The low-scoring defensive struggles had an adverse effect on attendance and gave an undue advantage to teams that relied on brute strength. The new rules opened-up the passing game and provided a boom to Coach Rockne and the Notre Dame football team. It introduced speed as a factor in football games and allowed Gipp to maximize his talents.

However, as Notre Dame began its spring session, Gipp's absence was having an effect on the team, "...No one is more enthusiastic over the 1920 getaway than head Coach Knute Rockne. He shed his hat and coat shortly after the squad reached the field and warmed up with the squad."

"The opening practice was featured by the absence of several stars who festooned the champion 1919 aggregation. There was no 'Dutch' Bergman to wiggle and squirm his way through a nest of tacklers or a George Gipp to hurl the oval from post to post with uncanny accuracy. The loss of a brace of halfbacks like Bergman and Gipp is a blow that would dishearten leaders less stout hearted than Rockne and Dorias."

By the end of spring practice on May 7, 1920 the football fortunes for Notre Dame had improved considerably. "Coach Rockne brings his spring football practice to a close this afternoon with a big scrimmage between the yearlings and the varsity. Because of the fact that scores of fans have been watching the work of promising candidates for berths on the varsity, this mixup will be witnessed by teen observers who are anxious to get a line on the Gold and Blue 1920 prospects."

"The reinstatement of George Gipp, big halfback who stirred on the eleven last year, has caused the varsity stock to soar. Gipp, who was elected to pilot the varsity next fall, was expelled from school because of scholarship conditions and has been reinstated after a petition signed by businessmen was delivered to President Burns."

On the following day, the regulars defeated the freshmen 7–0 while Gipp and Bernie Kirk watched the game from the sidelines.

On May 10, 1920 Gipp made his debut as a member of the varsity baseball team in a game against the Michigan Aggies. Gipp drove in the winning run in a 11–10 game by walking with the bases loaded in the bottom of the ninth after Michigan had fought back to tie the game at 10. Arch Ward wrote that Gipp's return to baseball brightened prospects for Notre Dame's baseball team.

"George Gipp's return to the baseball squad has given the club a decided stimulus and the Gold and Blue mentor (Dorias was the baseball coach) speaks optimistically over the outcome with Valparaiso. Gipp, sensational halfback of the Champion Notre Dame football eleven, made his debut in baseball this season last Saturday and played a big part in the victory over the Aggies. Gipp carries all the attributes of a first class outfielder. He is much faster than the average man of his size. Once George gets underway he's a tidal wave and a Sahara sandstorm rolled into one. He stops at nothing, but drives on blindly in pursuit of the ball. It is at the stick, however, where Gipp will lead most valuable assistance. Although the big grid star garnered but one hit in his inaugural appearance this spring, he packs a devastating wallop in his bat that is certain to spread havoc along the route of university pitchers the rest of the season."

But Gipp's baseball career was shortlived at Notre Dame. In their next game, on May 17th, against Valparaiso there was no mention of Gipp in the newspaper account of the contest. Notre Dame defeated Valparaiso, 2–0 behind the one-hit pitching of Johnny Mohardt.

Gipp was not to play another baseball game for the Notre Dame baseball club. Shortly after a game against Iowa, on May 21st, Gipp quit the club and accepted an offer by the University of Detroit to play football. Pete Bahan, who ran out of eligibility with Notre Dame, also accepted an offer to play for the University of Detroit. Gipp was upset with the way he was treated at Notre Dame, and to get revenge he decided to accept the offer from the other school.

Gipp felt there was just too much pressure at Notre Dame. There was pressure to perform on the athletic field. There was pressure to maintain a standard of conduct and there was considerable pressure in the classroom. Gipp was free-spirited and did not like others telling him what he could and what he couldn't do. He saw nothing wrong with gambling and poolroom hustles despite the protest from high-brows in South Bend. Gambling and the men it attracted to the game were abhorrent to Coach Rockne, but Gipp saw them as a necessary part of the game. The University of Detroit was not about to place any restriction on Gipp's lifestyle. That, and the promise of cash payments made their offer too tempting to refuse.

Gipp was not the only Notre Dame star to defect to another school. Bernie Kirk, who formed the second half of the "Gipp to Kirk" passing combination which lit up the scoreboard during the 1919 season, accepted an offer from the University of Michigan.

For the summer, Gipp accepted an offer from Joe Swetish to play baseball for a Buick Motor Car Company factory team. The factory leagues had a high quality of baseball. It could be considered favorably comparable to the Triple-A level of the minor leagues. Many players who participated in the factory league went on to major league stardom. There was Hazen "Kiki" Cuyler, who starred for the Buick I team before later becoming a great outfielder for the Chicago Cubs.

One of Gipp's teammates, Joe Collard remembered playing with both Cuyler and Gipp. "Cuyler could do it all—speed hitting, excellent throwing arm. He used to come often during those days in Flint and ask me if I thought he could make it. I used to tell him with his talent the only place to go was up," Collard said.

"George was a most likeable fellow, always smiling, very good-natured and humorous. He was a fine outfielder and an excellent base runner. He was very deceptive in his movements, giving you the impression of not trying, but he had such fine coordination that he always seemed to do the job, getting under fly balls or stealing a base with nothing to spare. He always seemed to know just how much effort was needed for the situation. I hear it was the same when he played football."

As he played baseball throughout the summer, Gipp began to miss Notre Dame. One time Joe Savinni asked him how he was going to do at Notre Dame in the fall. Gipp said, "It's really going to show them something this year," forgetting that he had accepted an offer from the University of Detroit.

Gipp also received an offer from the Canton Bulldogs professional football team which was reported in the August 20th edition of the *Flint Journal.*

"...We are pleased to report that George Gipp plans to play with Dort-Lakeside on Sunday against the Saginaw semipros. Gipp, the Notre Dame star who makes all the uniforms look small, showed the patrons of last Sunday that he has the Gimp and will be a big attraction, particularly with Copper Country fans. The Calumet-Laurium Club, which he was with last year, wired him to come for a tie-breaking game with Keweenaw come next Sunday, but he turned the offer down.

"Several interests have approached Gipp about playing football this fall. Being of the Notre Dame Club, he will probably return to college about September 25. He is, however, wavering whether or not he will drop his law courses for industrial pursuits." "Flint has a good chance at gaining his gridiron services as has Jim Thorpe, who offered him several hundred dollars a game both last summer and this."

It is clear that a bidding war of sorts was under way. Rockne was furious at the prospect of losing Gipp. He heard the reports about the University of Detroit and decided to send Gus Dorias up to Michigan to fetch Gipp. In later years, Dorias related an account of the incident to former football player Tilly Voss.

"I walked into Rock's office ready to go to work in the year of 1920 and Rock says, 'Gus, don't unpack. Get on a train and go to Detroit. Get Gipp back here.' I understand he's playing with some school called Detroit College or the University of Detroit. He's there with Bernie Kirk and a couple of others we had last year. I don't care too much about them except maybe Kirk, but get Gipp back or don't you come back because neither you nor I will have a job if we don't get Gipp. *He's* our team.' "

"Well," Dorias said, "I get up here and ask where Detroit College or where the University of Detroit is. I'm told it's down on Jefferson Avenue. I go there but I don't see any campus or anything that looks like a football field. They tell me the team practices at a place called Belle Isle. I'd never heard of it and don't know where it is, so I get in a cab at Rock's expense."

"I'm driven across a bridge to a big field where two or three outfits are practicing. I make inquiries. One chap tells me, 'That's the Heralds over there.' Another says, 'Those fellows are the Records.' "

"Where's the University of Detroit?" Dorias asked.

He was pointed to another section of the park where the Detroit team was practicing.

"I strolled over and stood at a respectful distance. I saw Gipp in the backfield running through plays. A fellow named "Bingo" Brown is the coach. When the practice is over I move closer and Gipp sees me."

"George," I said, "What on earth are you doing up here?"

"Going to school, Gus," Gipp said.

"But why up here, don't you know you're going to be an All-American selection this season if you play for Notre Dame?"

"But, Gus, I'm always ineligible after the football season at Notre Dame. I want to play basketball and baseball. I'm eligible up here for all sports. I want to go to school where I can play."

"Listen, George" Dorias said, "They held a board meeting last week and they ruled you would be eligible for everything at Notre Dame. You've got to go back with me. It's my job if you don't. Rock says its his job, too."

George Gipp told Dorias that he shouldn't worry and that he would return to Notre Dame. On September 5th, Gipp left Flint and boarded a train that took him to Calumet after a brief stop in Chicago. During the layover in Chicago, Gipp ran into Ojay Larson.

"It was early evening," Larson said, "and as he had not eaten his dinner he invited me into a restaurant for dessert and coffee while he had something to eat. While we talked, he told me he was on his way back from Flint and was scheduled to take the next train to Calumet. At that moment he was still undecided on whether to complete his trip to Calumet or change his ticket for one to Indianapolis. He informed me that he had met a young lady with whom he was enamored and that she was a strong factor in his dilemma. He said it was now costing him about $65.00 a month to call her long distance. Anyway, he said, if he did decide finally to go to Calumet, it would be his last visit there," Larson said.

Gipp returned to Calumet and spent nearly a month with family and friends. While he was there he visited Dr. R.C. Roche, who tried to get Gipp to allow him to remove his infected tonsils before going back to South Bend. Gipp was nervous about the operation and decided to skip it. He boarded a train for South Bend late in September.

The 1920 Football Season

As Coach Rockne led his team out for the first practice session in the fall, several star players were missing. During the first week of practice *The South Bend Tribune* reporter Arch Ward spent more time writing about those who didn't show up.

September 16, 1920

"...When Coach Rockne sent his Notre Dame football squad through its initial practice on Cartier Field yesterday afternoon the faces of Trafton and Maddigan at center; Malone, Pearson, Bahan, Bergman and Mohardt at halfback; Miller and Slackford at fullback, Degree at tackle and Bernie Kirk at end did not appear. This throws a big task to Coach Rockne's shoulders: that of developing practically a new team for the stiff schedule arranged this season.

"Mohardt had been hailed as the coming star in the backfield while Kirk was given a beret on last year's All-American eleven by eastern critics who saw him play against Army. It is uncertain to date whether or not either of these athletes will re-enter the university."

September 17, 1920

"...Rockne is standing on the doormat of a season beset with difficulties. Confronted with a heavy schedule and with only a relic of his whirlwind 1919 eleven to begin with, Rockne sees an insurmountable hurdle in the path of an undefeated season."

"Prospects were brightened somewhat yesterday by the appearance of Johnny Mohardt in a uniform when the roll was called at practice. Mohardt is one of last year's halfbacks who is counted upon for great things on the eleven this year. Larson and E. Degree, last year's freshmen stars, also reported yesterday. Gipp, Kirk and Smith are the athletes yet to make their appearances."

Gipp finally returned to Notre Dame around September 27th, when he arrived he found that he was suspended from the football team because of poor grades. In addition, Bahan was also suspended.

September 22, 1920

"...Prospects for another champion football team at Notre Dame were given a backspin yesterday afternoon when the university faculty declared George Gipp and Leonard Bahan, stellar members of the 1919 eleven, ineligible for further competition under Gold and Blue colors. Grid stock at Cartier Field sank to moody depths when the fateful news was whispered about."

"The loss of Gipp and Bahan complicates Coach Rockne's task of developing a backfield that can penetrate the defense of such powerful teams as Nebraska, the Army, Purdue and Indiana."

Rockne was extremely dismayed at Gipp's suspension. He had already authorized Dorias to go to Michigan and bring Gipp back. Dorias had promised Gipp that he would be allowed to play football and not have to worry about his grades. It is clear that a confrontation between the football team and the faculty was headed for a showdown.

The most likely reason for Gipp's suspension relates to his early exit from Notre Dame in the spring. When he left to play baseball after accepting the offer from the University of Detroit, Gipp had neglected to finish his school work at Notre Dame for the spring semester. Gipp had failed to take any of his final exams and this caused the faculty to declare him ineligible.

On the day after the faculty declared Gipp ineligible, Notre Dame held it's first scrimmage with the freshmen. Even though the varsity was able to perform quite well, scoring at least five touchdowns in a limited scrimmage, it was clear that the outlook for the Notre Dame football team was not good. The team appeared uncoordinated all throughout the scrimmage.

September 23, 1920

"...Coach Rockne makes no attempt to conceal a big disappointment over the condition of the varsity squad. The usually optimistic tutor exuded gloom as thick as cheese on toasted crackers last night. At times during the scrimmage his men showed flashes of form, but for the most part the workout developed nothing but enormous gobs of pessimism. Fumbles were numerous and mental blunders were frequent. Unless some unforseen circumstance throws a harpoon into the situation,

Notre Dame will have to perk up to humble the scrappy Kalamazoo eleven which will exhibit here a week from Saturday."

Ticket sales were being hurt, as the suspension of Gipp and the poor performance on the practice field made it difficult to sell season tickets. On September 24th, Notre Dame suffered a second blow of bad news, as Bernie Kirk officially notified Rockne that he would not be attending Notre Dame.

September 24, 1920

"...The open season for the football jinx is in full blast and the Notre Dame campus abounds with the deadliest of menaces. No sooner had Gold and Blue fans recovered from the shock of Gipp's and Bahan ineligibility then came word that Bernie Kirk, stellar end of the 1919 eleven, will not return to Notre Dame this fall. Kirk's withdrawal means the total wreck of last seasons famous 'Gipp to Kirk' scoring machine.

"Official announcement of Kirk's withdrawal was made yesterday afternoon following a telephone communication between the stellar wing man and Coach Rockne. Kirk had decided to enter Michigan University and will don Wolverine togs in the near future.

"Irresponsible student rumors that Kirk was offered big inducements to enter Michigan because of his athletic prowess are groundless. Kirk entered Michigan because his sister lives near Ann Arbor, making it convenient."

Even though Kirk told Rockne that he enrolled at the University of Michigan to be near his sister, the allegation that the school bribed the star end is not beyond the realm of possibility. When Dorias visited Gipp on the University of Detroit practice field during the summer, Kirk was also on the field. Dorias remembered that at the time it appeared that the University of Michigan was after Kirk.

The loss of the great passing combination made Notre Dame's prospects for the upcoming season perilous at best. Rockne had to find a way to get Gipp back in the fold.

On Monday, September 27th, season tickets were mailed to 1,500 fans as Rockne tried to straighten out the teams problems. Ticket sales were behind that pace of the 1919 season, as the loss of Gipp, Kirk and Bahan made fans skeptical about the season. On the day before, Notre Dame's first opponent, Kalamazoo defeated the Michigan Aggies. Notre Dame had scheduled the Kalamazoo team because it wanted a "softy" to start the season. When Kalamazoo turned out to be much tougher than expected, fans began to have fear an end to the long unbeaten string.

To get Gipp reinstated, Rockne asked the faculty board to approve an oral exam. This was highly irregular, but the school administration, pressured by townspeople and alumni agreed and let Gipp take an oral exam. Rockne spent the afternoon of September 28th, pacing back and forth, as Gipp was brought in to answer questions. After a long two hour hearing, the faculty announced that Gipp had passed the exams he had missed.

September 29, 1920
"...The ineligibility of George Gipp, all-western halfback of Notre Dame University, caused by his

recent suspension was cleared up at a meeting of the faculty athletic board held yesterday afternoon. Gipp, who returned to school last week, was granted a hearing before the board, and on a presentation of a statement of satisfactory work in his June examinations from the law department his disqualification was removed."

"Gipp was in uniform yesterday afternoon and his presence radiated enthusiasm. Such a display of pepper has not been seen Cartier Field this fall as was evidenced Tuesday afternoon. Notre Dame fandom is fizzing and foaming like an uncorked bottle of pop in anticipation of another whirlwind gridiron campaign. Thursday evening's big pep-meeting in Washington Hall is only a merry prelude of what will follow."

"In all probability Gipp will start against Kalamazoo Saturday. If his bullet like passes to Anderson and Barry Tuesday afternoon are a criterion of what the season is to produce, Notre Dame will steam-roller its way to another western football title as it did a year ago. The pennant route, to be sure, is long and rugged, but with another week or two of practice the big Gold and Blue eleven should function like a well tuned machine. Rockne has instilled the doughboy spirit into his pupils — one for all and all for one."

"No one is more pleased over Gipp's reinstatement than he himself. Gipp loves the gridiron, and he loves Notre Dame and unless our forecast goes amiss he will be a big aid in helping his mates attain unprecedented heights this autumn. With the veteran Brandy at quarterback and Mohardt, Barry and Coughlin as halfbacks Notre Dame's backfield doesn't look so anemic as reported."

Gipp's reinstatement had to be a final blow to those who wanted to upgrade the statue of Notre Dame as an institution of higher learning. Here was a student who openly breached all the rules and yet he was still allowed to compete while wearing the school's colors. Football had assumed a great place of importance at Notre Dame, never to be dislodged. As Rockne weighed his chances he realized that playing without Gipp would inevitably lead to defeat. Rockne was a great coach. His ability to bring a team that was physically overmatched to victory after victory testifies to his coaching ability. Gipp was a frustration and a puzzlement to Rockne, who vowed that no single player would ever so dominate the Notre Dame program ever again. He wanted a team with no single star. That's why he was so pleased to develop the four-back offense of "The Four Horsemen," a few years after Gipp was gone.

Coach Rockne was in a jam when the 1920 season began. While he was well stocked with linemen, his backfield was depleted. The day after Gipp was reinstated, another backfield man was injured in practice.

September 30, 1920

"...A rapidly dropping temperature failed to cool the enthusiasm of the Notre Dame football squad Wednesday in preparation for the opening game with Kalamazoo Saturday and the varsity men smothered the freshies under an avalanche of touchdowns that disclosed surprising power. Bolstered by the presence of Gipp, Captain Coughlin's bunch ran rough shod over a rather anemic yearling aggregation.

"The list of backfield reserves was decreased by an untimely injury to Walsh in scrimmage yesterday. Walsh replaced Coughlin as halfback after the scrimmage was well under way and he was injured on the first play. He has been hampered by a lame knee hurt on Cartier Field a year ago and it is feared he will be unable to enter the Kalamazoo contest. With Mohardt and Walsh out of the lineup, Rockne's number of halfbacks has dwindled to an alarming degree. Gipp, Barry and Coughlin are the only halfbacks of known ability in the fold.

"It was easy for the varsity backs to rip off long runs through the opposing team with the forwards opening big holes. Foreward passes, Gipp to Kiley and Gipp to Anderson, worked successfully on several occasions. Gipp ran 60 yards for a touchdown on an off-tackle play just before Rockne sent in a flock of substitutes to even up the contest."

The 1920 season inaugurated several new rules. These new rules helped establish the passing game and eliminate rough play. Rockne spent several hours discussing the new regulations. In an article on October 1st, noted sportswriter Walter Camp discussed the new regulations and the effect they would have on the game.

October 1, 1920
"...There never was a more interesting interpretation meeting of football officials and coaches than that held in New York last week. There never was a stronger body of football men gathered together, and the result was a very thorough going over the question of how the new laws should be fairly interpreted. It is true the

changes in the laws of the game were few but those few are of very vital importance and the way in which these will be interpreted on the field of play makes every difference in the world to the coaches who now are engaged in settling their players and developing their methods."

"The two most important features are the addition under the rule regarding unnecessary roughness — a practice which has been gaining ground and which might become a serious menace to the game. This practice is variously called 'clipping', 'cutting down from behind,' and 'brutal play.' It has received attention but no one up to the night of the interpretation meeting has ever been able to give a definition that would cover what should be regarded as unnecessary roughness and yet at the same time not interfere with perfectly legitimate and unobjectionable methods."

The wording in effect means that cutting down from behind — that is, throwing the body laterally from behind against that part of the leg or legs of another player who is not carrying the ball — would be considered unnecessary roughness.

The tactic of clipping had come into increasing favor by coaches all over the country. It was used primarily by tight ends, split ends and flankers to open the way for running backs. It was highly effective, but it was also very dangerous. When Gipp played defense he was victimized by this style of blocking numerous times. The "legal" clipping ruined the careers of many players as the block to the back of the legs would cause many knee injuries.

"...The other rule which took nearly an hour of discussion is that regarding the player in motion. This relates to so-called 'Shift' plays, and also to plays where a man starts on the run diagonally towards his own goal before the ball is put in play. The latter has always been sufficiently clear, but two officials are now entrusted with the watching of it. The other is a shift play where men change from one position to another before the ball is put in play, has always been a bone of contention and somewhat difficult for officials to rule upon. The rule provides that a man must come to a stop after he makes a shift so that he is not in motion when the ball is snapped."

These shift plays have developed more largely in the south, middle west and Pacific coast than in the east. And for the last two years, double and triple shifts have been used. After a time it came to be apparent that there was a tendency to use some of the additional shifts, and so-called hike plays for the purpose of drawing the opponents offside. There is a rule in the books which already forbids any motion made with the intent to draw the opponents offside. Teams were warned last year that if they used such hike or shift play, and it was suspected they were for this purpose, they would be penalized.

This left the matter somewhat in the air, for every coach who used shift plays became excited when there was any insinuation was no such intention, and that if the opponents came offside. They were doing it in an attempt to beat the play.

The new rule set up penalties when officials believed that the play was designed to draw opponents offside. It also set up a system to regulate the type of motion that could be used and the number of men who could be put in motion before the snap.

As Notre Dame readied itself for Kalamazoo, the reinsertion of Gipp bolstered the hopes of the Blue and Gold. "Gipp's presence will insert a devastating smash to the Notre Dame attack, an assault which is bound to spread havoc among the western pennant contenders this fall. Should line plays and end runs fail to materialize the team, with Gipp in the lineup, can unveil its overhead attack and the opponents will be forced back towards their own goal. Rockne will strive to defeat the visitors with straight football. Open work will be held in reserve for Nebraska two weeks from today."

October 2, 1920

Led by Gipp, Notre Dame racked up a 39–0 win against Kalamazoo. Gipp gained 183 yards in 16 rushes, his best running effort in his career. He barely played one half of football as Notre Dame built up a commanding lead early in the game.

"Machine-like in its coordination and thoroughly bulldogish in its fighting spirit, the Notre Dame eleven vanquished Kalamazoo Saturday and gained a flying start towards another western championship. More than 5,000 fans, the largest gathering that every attended an opening engagement at Notre Dame, were present.

"The visitors fought hard and long. Their tricky end runs were solved early in the gaze by Coach Rockne's athletes and their widely heralded overhead attack, save for the fourth quarter when the short passes were executed successfully, failed to materialize."

After the teams exchanged punts, Notre Dame began driving with its running attack. "Gipp started the march to the first touchdown with a nine yard sprint off tackle. Brandy hit the center of the line for a first down. Gipp plowed tackle for ten more and Barry broke away for 25. With the ball on the ten-yard line, Wynne hammered his way over the goal line for a touchdown. Gipp missed in the try for extra point."

After the defense held, "...long runs by Gipp and Barry soon placed the ball on the Kazoo 20-yard line. Notre Dame missed signals and Barry was held for no gain. Notre Dame was handed a five yard penalty for an offside play. Barry and Gipp nibbled at the line for short gains, placing the ball on the five-yard line. After this Gipp bolted through tackle for the second touchdown."

In the third quarter Gipp led Notre Dame to another touchdown with a 28 yard run and a 20 yard pass to Kiley. After Barry scored a touchdown to give Notre Dame an 18–0 lead, Gipp and many of his first string mates were pulled from the game by Rockne. The second stringers extended the lead.

"The Notre Dame forwards cut jagged holes in the Kalamazoo defense and Barry scored another touchdown before the third quarter was well under way. Kalamazoo opened up its aerial stuff late in the period and managed to keep possession of the ball for several minutes. Notre Dame scored its third touchdown of the period just before time was called when Kasper, a substitute for Gipp, broke through tackle for ten yards.

"A second string lineup performed for Notre Dame throughout the fourth quarter. Stellar offensive work by Mohardt featured the final round. Time and again he shook off a legion of tacklers and squirmed his way for 15 and 20 yard runs." Roger Kiley, who replaced Bernie Kirk, turned out to be a big star of the game. But Kiley had a bad case of the jitters and on Notre Dame's first possession Gipp hit him perfectly when he was wide open. Kiley dropped the ball.

"If a gate had been open I would have run to Chicago," Kiley said.

"There was no way out, and I came back to the huddle. George said to Brandy, 'Joe, call it again.' Joe did. I caught the next pass and several others. After the game George said to me, 'Roger, come out fifteen minutes early next week and we'll get better acquainted, and we'll stand them on their heads.' "

The next game, on October 9th was against Western Normal. This was another of the early season "softies" that Rockne liked to set up. Throughout the week Rockne had to battle overconfidence. "...Since the great showing of the team in the Kalamazoo game optimism is popping out from all corners of the field. Despite the easy triumph of Notre Dame over Western Normal a year ago, Coach Rockne is anticipating rugged opposition from the Wolverine teachers. This is another year and a battle from Saturday's opponent would not be the first upset of a season bristling with sterling opposition.

"Saturday's game will be the first test this season for Western Normal. The squad has been practicing diligently for three weeks in preparation for the contest and you can rest assured that the teachers will put up a good fight. Notre Dame is slated to win by a wide margin."

Much of this was Rockne's attempt to get his team ready for the opposition. Rockne believed that the best way to motivate his team was to "hype" the opposition. One of his great achievements as a coach was that his team was rarely surprised or upset by the opposition. Notre Dame was rarely beaten by an inferior opponent.

October 9, 1920
In its second game, Notre Dame posted its second decisive victory, defeating, Western Normal 41–0.

"...With a host of substitutes in the lineup Notre Dame romped away from Western State Normal and piled up a 41–0 score.

"Notre Dame had no trouble at any stage of the contest. Gipp dashed down the field for touchdowns on two occasions only to be called back on account of offside play by his mates and Kasper added another touchdown, in the third quarter, but the play was thrown out for the same reason. The Normal team failed to make first downs except on penalties, so rugged was the Gold and Blue defense.

"Notre Dame relied solely on straight football for gains while the Wolverines banked on an overhead assault for advances. In nearly every instance the visitors forward passes were smeared by the Notre Dame backs.

"Stellar work by the Irish linemen featured the contest. Time and again Coughlin, Anderson, Smith and Shaw bolted through the Normal bulwark and buried the runner for a loss. The attack of the tutors failed to dent the Notre Dame line. It was easy for Gipp, Mohardt and the other backfield fliers to rip off long runs with the linesmen cutting jagged gashes in the opponents defense."

Gipp was very successful on the ground, gaining 123 yards on 14 carries.

For the next week, Notre Dame was to face its first real test of the season. The Nebraska Cornhuskers always provided tough opposition for Notre Dame. As Notre Dame left for Lincoln, Rockne felt optimistic.

October 14, 1920

"...Rockne feels sure he will wallop the Cornhuskers by a bigger margin than he did last year. His aggregation is outweighed man for man but "Rock" isn't the fellow who crows about a little weight. He wants men who can play football with the fighting spirit in them and are able to act on the spur of the moment. He has one of the greatest squads ever sent out from the Irish institution and one which should beat Nebraska, Valparaiso, Purdue and the Army."

October 16, 1920

"...Notre Dame came from behind in Saturday's battle with the powerful Cornhuskers and won a well-earned victory by the score of 16–7."

"It was as impressive triumph and the gameness of the Visitors delighted the 10,000 old grads and students who crowded the park. Fighting and snarling like a bunch of cornered wildcats, and smarting under the sting of the opponent's touchdowns, the Notre Dame eleven unbelted an attack and could not be denied."

"The performance of George Gipp, halfback of Notre Dame featured the game. Time and again the big backfield star broke through the Nebraska line for big gains. His forward passes were instrumental in scoring both Notre Dame touchdowns. Early in the second period, Gipp broke through the entire Nebraska team for a 55 yard run and a touchdown, but the play was called back and Notre Dame penalized 15 yards."

The first quarter was a defensive struggle as both teams had trouble with rainy, wet conditions. Midway through the quarter Notre Dame drove down to the Nebraska five-yard line but turned the ball over on downs when a line plunge failed on fourth down. Nebraska was unable to move the ball. A Notre Dame lineman blocked an attempted punt, with the ball bouncing out of the end zone. This safety gave Notre Dame a 2–0 lead. But, Notre Dame was unable to hold the lead, as a bad punt by Gipp gave the Cornhuskers the ball in Notre Dame territory. The Cornhuskers drove a down the field and scored a touchdown at the end of the first quarter.

After two drives in the second quarter didn't produce any yardage, Rockne was tempted to replace some of his regulars. He wanted to replace Chet Wynne, who was a friend of Gipp's with Bob Phelan. During a break in the game Rockne apparently was getting ready to pull Wynne when Gipp tried to talk him out of it.

"Rock — how about Chetter?"

"No," Rockne replied.

"Give him another chance," Gipp pleaded.

Wynne had fumbled the ball several times in the game against Western Normal. He also had dropped a potential touchdown pass, yet Gipp thought the back had a good deal of ability. His confidence in Wynne undoubtedly saved his career. Rockne put him back in the lineup and was rewarded when the back began making big plays. In the second quarter his block led to Gipp's long touchdown run that was called back. Undaunted, Gipp lead his team down the field for the score which gave Notre Dame the lead.

Notre Dame opened up its aerial attack, and a series of passes, Gipp to E. Anderson, placed the ball on Nebraska's ten-yard line. Wynne cut through center for two yards, and another pass, Gipp to E. Anderson, put the ball on the one-yard line, from where Brandy promptly drove through center for a touchdown.

After a scoreless third quarter, Gipp lead Notre Dame to its final touchdown of the game with a long pass to Norman Barry which put the ball just inside the Cornhusker 20-yard line. From there, Gipp scored on a run after faking the pass. The score gave Notre Dame some breathing room and the Blue and Gold went on to complete a 16–7 victory.

It was a good day for Gipp in that he led Notre Dame to the win, but it was a bad game statistically. He rushed the ball 15 times for 70 yards and completed only 6 of 20 passes for another 117 yards. He was hurt by penalties when he ran and dropped passes when he threw.

Several Nebraska players remember Gipp as the best player on the field.

"I would call George one of the greatest. He was an outstanding back that day, and in those days we had a great defensive team. In the game the year before against us he made most of his yardage against Ray Lyman, the greatest defensive tackle Nebraska ever had — the same Lyman who later was an All-Pro Scherer.

Clarence Swanson, who played left end for the Cornhuskers said Gipp was the best passer and runner he had ever seen. Swanson remembered that Gipp was involved in a memorable trick play.

"Rockne dreamed up this fake play that was perfectly legal," Swanson said. "The Notre Dame players advised Referee Quigley that at a certain time they would fake an injury but did not want time called out. They lined up with seven men on the line; their center, Larson, however, feigned an injury, dropped down and lay on his stomach. Suddenly he turned over and threw the ball back to Gipp, and he went around us for a touchdown. We didn't even see him until he got past us. Unfortunately for them, however, Johnny Mohardt, who was the other halfback, was caught for clipping, and the play was called back and Notre Dame was penalized 15 yards. Gipp's words were, 'Don't mind, Johnny, we'll soon have another one,' and it wasn't long before Gipp came through."

The next game on Notre Dame's schedule was against Valparaiso. Many people in South Bend were looking past Valparaiso and ahead to the Army game. For Coach Rockne, it was a test of his motivational ability as a leader. It was difficult to get his team ready for the game. When the Notre Dame train arrived back in South Bend, Rockne found that many players were nursing injuries.

October 18, 1920
"...Battered and bruised from their conflict with the heavy Nebraska eleven, the Notre Dame athletes took things easy Monday afternoon. A field talk by Coach Rockne and a short signal drill" was the only activity.

"Kiley, end, and Degree, guard, were unable to report for yesterday's workout. Kiley suffered a nervous shock as a result of an injury in the Nebraska game and Degree has a dislocated knee." Notre Dame had set up a new grandstand to take advantage of the great interest in the Valparaiso game. It increased the price of general admission tickets and tacked on a surcharge for season ticket holders.

"If the advance sale of tickets is a criterion, the largest crowd that ever attended a contest on Cartier Field will see Notre Dame play Valparaiso Saturday. Persons holding season tickets and desiring reserved seats will be charged fifty cents. The season ticket and the seat stub must be presented at the gate for admittance. The reserved section will be the new grand stand on the west side of the field. Temporary bleachers will be erected at either end of the field to accommodate general admission patrons.

"Rated as one of the heaviest teams on the gridiron, Coach Keegan's men have established a record that discloses surprising speed. In the three games played by the neighboring eleven, it has rung up 136 points against 21 for its rivals. Harvard, which defeated Valpo 21–0, is the only team that has desecrated the team's goal this fall. Measured by the yardstick of comparative weights, the visiting team will carry a wide margin over Rockne's clan. From tackle to tackle, Valparaiso averages over 200 pounds while Notre Dame averages about 176 pounds."

October 19, 1920

Notre Dame's injury list expanded as quarterback, Joe Brandy had a dislocated shoulder.

"...Unless Notre Dame's list of cripples improves more rapidly than expected, Valpo will confront only a torn and twisted shell of the sturdy array that overthrew the Cornhuskers at Lincoln last week. But the fighting spirit of the Irish is still rampant and it will take more than a horny headed jinx to put Rockne's clan out of the running.

"Joe Brandy is the latest star who has been plucked out of the lineup. Brandy was injured in the Nebraska game and an examination Monday revealed a dislocated shoulder. His injury is not serious however, and he will probably be in shape for Saturday's game, but in view of the West Point contest next week Rockne may keep him on the sidelines.

"Chet Grant will probably get his first real test of the year against Valparaiso. He played in the final moments of the Nebraska game, but it was difficult to appraise his worth in that short space of time. He demonstrated, however, that he is as fast afoot as ever and he moved the team in a sprightly manner.

"In its victory over Nebraska, Notre Dame proved it will be a hard team to stop. Rockne has equipped the men with a variety of plays that bewilder opponents. His wizardry was behind every move of the Notre Dame team at Lincoln. A fast attack is always a vital factor in shaping the outcome of important football games, but Notre Dame is showing its superiority in other respects as well. On defense, for instance, the

Irish functioned like an old Swiss clock replete with well oiled mechanism."

October 23, 1920
"...If Notre Dame beats Valparaiso today, enthusiasm over the Army game will be rife next week. The Army has swept everything before it to date and is heralded as the strongest eleven that has represented the officers in a decade.

"Army scouts at Lincoln admitted they feared Notre Dame more than any team on their schedule. They said they will consider the season a glorious success if they triumph over Notre Dame, whatever be the outcome of the struggle with Navy.

"Reports emanating from Gotham State that many newspaper experts will flock to the game in the hope of finding material for their mythical All-American eleven. For the first time since Notre Dame has invaded the East it is being recognized as a team of champion potentiality. Gipp, Brandy, Coughlin, H. Anderson, and Smith will be the cynosure of critical eyes when the two teams tangle on the wind-sprayed plains of the Hudson."

Nearly 8,000 fans jammed into Cartier Field for the Valparaiso game on October 23, 1920. Because Army scouts were in the stands checking every move by Notre Dame, Coach Rockne started his second stringers. It was a move that almost backfired playing for the Irish. It was off that combination that Valpo scored three points on a pretty field goal by Echard from the 35-yard line. Rockne rushed his regular's into the fray when Valpo advanced the ball to the local's 20-yard line early in the second period. The regular lineup looked like a barrier of steel and concrete to Keegan's Men and they were unable to proceed further on their goalward march."

After turning the ball over on downs, Gipp punted the ball out of danger as the half ended with Notre Dame behind 3-0. As the players left the field, many fans were upset with Rockne. By keeping his best players off the field, many thought that he was needlessly risking the game. If Valparaiso had scored on its second quarter drive the game might have turned out quite differently. But, with the first stringers back on the field Notre Dame romped in the second half, winning 28-3.

"Standing head and shoulders above every player on the field was George Gipp. Gipp's meteoric run of 38 yards for a touchdown, in the fourth period through the entire Valpo team was the feature performance. No less praiseworthy was his crash through tackle for Notre Dame's first touchdown, when he carried four opponents on his back over the goal line. He picked holes in the enemy's defense uncanny precision. His passing and punting gained many yards for his.

"Valpo was exhausted when the game ended, while Notre Dame, due to the frequent substitutions was conspicuously fresh. The final whistle found Valpo opposing a lineup composed largely of third string players. Rockne gave the West Point scouts, who were in attendance, an opportunity to see the wealth of material he has developed."

The real reason Rockne used second and third string players during much of the Valparaiso game was to keep Army scouts from finding out what was in the

Notre Dame playbook. He often used this tactic when he knew that an upcoming opponent had sent scouts to Notre Dame games.

The Army game was the most important game on Notre Dame's schedule. For Army, it was a chance to avenge last year's defeat and an opportunity to continue an undefeated season. The Cadets had romped through their 1920 schedule, scoring 158 points while giving up only 13. Included among the Army victories was three shutouts: Marshall College, 40–0 Union, 35–0: and Middlebury, 29–0. The Cadets viewed Notre Dame as the most formidable opponent on its schedule. In the newspaper account following the Valparaiso game Arch Ward wrote that the Notre Dame-Army contest would determine which region of the country had the best football team.

October 25, 1920

"...Dependent on the wizardry of a strategic Coach and the brilliancy of one of its greatest teams, the west will pit its best against the east when Notre Dame and the Army glare at each other on the banks of the Hudson Saturday. It will be the first test of the comparative strength of eastern and western football. Harvard, in defeating Valparaiso, scored a triumph for the east, but the Valpo outfit is not a fair representative of this section of the country.

"The Army, which was edged out by Notre Dame, Syracuse and the Navy a year ago, is coming back gloriously this fall and has walloped everything in its path by overwhelming scores. The West Point reserves drubbed Tufts while Notre Dame was lowering the titular aspirations of Valparaiso. Notre Dame is admittedly a leader in western football and will be backed up by friend and foe in its clash with the eastern pace setters this week."

"I can't see a weak spot on the team," remarked one of the West Point scouts who saw Notre Dame beat Valparaiso, "It's a remarkably well balanced eleven," the officer added.

"The two Army representatives also saw the Notre Dame-Nebraska game at Lincoln, from which we may infer that the Cadets are bending every effort to rise from the bog into which they have been plunged by defeats at the hands of Notre Dame. The Irish have won four of the six games played between the two teams. Every year Notre Dame unleashes some new fangled aerial attack that takes the officers by surprise, but the easterners will not be caught off their guard this autumn if careful scouting can prevent it."

"The West Point men who shared the press stand with us Saturday must have underlined with blue pencil in their notebooks that Valparaiso was outplayed and nonplused by a team that knows football of the most dangerous kind, an attack splendidly conceived and cleverly executed. Notre Dame, in its victory over Valparaiso, showed that it is as skilled in straight football as in open play. Nearly all of the local team's gains were made through openings furnished by Coughlin, H. Anderson, Larson, Smith and Shaw. It took the Gold and Blue men two quarters to get under way, but once they got a start they soon reduced the bulky brown clad Valpo athletes to quivering pulps."

The start of practice for the game against Army ushered in a long week of hype.

October 26, 1920

"...Bearing the unkempt aspects of drenched hens and crippled by the absence of Danny Coughlin, injured halfback the Notre Dame athletes scampered up and down a waterlogged field Monday in preparation for the big game with the Army Saturday. Coughlin has a wrenched knee and may be incapacitated from service for a week or more. He is recognized as one of the squad's most valuable substitute backfield men and his loss on the eve of the most important battle of the season would cripple Notre Dame considerably.

"Coach Rockne announced last night that the leftovers of the Varsity squad will play Lake Forest Academy at Lake Forest Saturday. About 23 players will be taken to West Point. There will be enough available second string men to present a strong lineup against the Lake Forest aggregation.

"No intersectional game that Notre Dame ever played is arousing the citizenry of South Bend and vicinity as the impending struggle with the Army. Not only the reputation of Notre Dame is at stake, but the entire west will share in Notre Dame's victory or defeat. Even the most radical opponent admits that Rockne's tribe is a pace setter for this section of the country. Critics and fans the country over recognize Notre Dame's superiority and it will be a choice array of football appraisers who will see the two teams fight each other to a sportive death Saturday. Not since the days when Rip Van Winkle stirred the Catskills with his little siesta have the hills around West Point been the center of so much attention.

"Saturday's game will mark Notre Dame's 14th contest with eastern teams. On all but three occasions the Gold and Blue men were returned victorious. The smoke screen with which Notre Dame has shielded its best plays thus far will be cast aside Saturday when Rockne will probably have the Gold and Blue disclose its best hand. Notre Dame has piled up many points this season by taking advantage of the other team's mistakes. It has withheld much of its more powerful stuff for the foes of the future. Rockne has developed the team gradually so when it goes to grips with the powerful Army eleven it will let go the best it owns in the way of trick plays and forward passes.

"Valparaiso more than lived up to its reputation Saturday, said Rockne last night. The Notre Dame athletes admit that the game was more bitterly contested than the score indicates. For two quarters the giant Keegan machine put up a stalwart defense and menacing attack that required the best the locals had to counteract. The visitors' sledge hammer blows at the line left an impression on the Notre Dame forwards that was still evident Monday afternoon. Most of the linesmen were nursing some sort of a scratch or bruise."

The team, however, will be in first rate condition for the Army game. Rockne has drilled his men splendidly in the fundamentals of play. The tackling, the interference, the running and the kicking in the Valpo contest was a decided improvement. The plays were run quickly and without hesitation. The attack was sustained and cohesive with adequate punch and speed. The defense, too, bespoke coaching of the highest order.

"Word has trickled into Notre Dame officialdom to prepare a defense for a human catapult in the person of French, giant fullback of the West Point team. In eastern circles he is pronounced the sensation of the season. Army opponents have had to play two men against French to stop his advances. Willhide, the pilot who directed the attack against Notre Dame a year ago, will again be at quarterback. It will be interesting to note the comparative capability of Willhide and Brandy."

October 27, 1920

"...Things looked bright on a foggy afternoon when the Notre Dame varsity snowed the yearlings (freshmen) under an avalanche of points that bespoke unlimited power yesterday afternoon. The gloom clouds were further dispelled by the word that Danny Coughlin, injured halfback, is rapidly improving and may be able to make the trip to West Point tomorrow.

"Rockne had not decided on the personnel of his squad last night. He stated that he will probably take 23 men. The party will leave South Bend at noon tomorrow and will reach West Point in time for a de-kinking exercise on the Army field Friday.

"The Notre Dame-West Point game will hold the calcium rays Saturday. In point of sterling competition it outshines anything scheduled for the day on American gridirons. In the east it has little rivalry for honors and it will more than overshadow the Chicago-Ohio State game billed for Stagg Field the same afternoon. Whereas the

Chicago affair will have a bearing only on the standing of the Big Ten conference, the West Point game will determine the rating of the entire west against the east.

"Saturday will be a great day for Notre Dame, win, lose or draw. The Gold and Blue athletes will find the critical eyes cast upon them from the first whistle to the end of the game. It will be the acid test for the entire team and for the coaching of Rockne and Halas in particular. To their credit it may be said that their popularity hasn't gone to their heads. They are still a complacent group of boys, thinking only to win the big battle. If they put it over, their fame will be immortal. If they fall, the west will be rated as inferior to the east in 1920 football."

"For George Gipp, halfback, the game, perhaps, means most of all. For him the contest will mean the making or breaking of an athlete of all-American potentiality. Recognized generally as the greatest backfield man in the west, Gipp is frequently mentioned as a candidate for the mythical All-Star team. His passing, punting, blocking and open field running will be carefully scrutinized Saturday. Gipp, however, is not the only Notre Dame athlete whose work will be carefully weighed by Gotham experts.

"Those who know the Notre Dame athletes are confident they will not fail in the pinch. They are going to West Point with their noodles deflated and don't rate themselves as a world-beating aggregation. They figure on doing just what Knute Rockne tells them they can do."

Rockne is going about the task of preparing for the Army in a very commonplace manner. The game hasn't disturbed him over much. Mobs, such as will see his team perform Saturday don't befuddle him, and neither does full face newspaper type. He and Coughlin are working to keep the excitement from throwing some of the younger members of the squad into delirium. Fortunately, it is not a difficult job. The Notre Dame boys are a simple crew, unaffected by their great record and quite unmoved by the tremendous hubbub."

On October 28th, Rockne and the Notre Dame team boarded a train and headed for the West Point Military Academy. Hundreds of fans and well-wishers sent them off with a rousing ovation. In his book about his life at Notre Dame, Hunk Anderson painted a vivid description of the long ride.

"Notre Dame had alloted about $4,000 for the trip, so we had to go second class," Anderson said. "We traveled by day coach; then that night we changed to Pullman. To cut down on expenses two guys were assigned to each of the lower and upper berths. Because of the high price of food on the train, we only had one full meal en route to the game, and for that we had to get off the train at Buffalo in order to find a cheap restaurant. Whenever any of the guys got hungry on the trip they'd jump off the train when it stopped, grab a quick bite, and be back before the train pulled out. None of us minded it though. We were just happy to go."

October 29, 1920

"...Tired and travel worn but optimistic over the outcome of their battle on the morrow, the Notre Dame football squad, 23 strong, reached West Point this morning after a 22-hour ride on the rails. The Hoosiers worked out on the Army field this afternoon and retired at an early hour for a long sleep."

Army Coach Daly ran his cadet eleven through a snappy practice today that bespoke great things for tomorrow. The Army tribe is in great condition and is determined to send the westerners home on the wrong end of the score. If their exhibition this afternoon is a criterion of their strength, they are powerful enough to turn the trick.

"This is perhaps the biggest mid-season day in the history of football. Scribes and fans from all corners of New York state are flocking here for tomorrow's battle, which, to a large degree will determine the standing of eastern and western football this autumn.

"For the boys of Uncle Sam's greatest military school tomorrow will be a gala day. In addition to the football game, which ranks as the most important on their schedule, the cadets will drill on the parade grounds for the thousands of visitors before the contest and the annual military ball in the evening. An invitation has been extended to the Notre Dame athletes to attend the social function, but the South Bend men are scheduled to leave here at 6:30 p.m.

"Opinions on the outcome of the game vary from a victory by a small margin for Notre Dame to a 20–0 triumph for the Army. The Cadets are known to have the strongest aggregation that has represented them in years and they are ready to back their team to the limit. Most wagers have been recorded at even money, although a few instances of 10 to 8 odds on West Point have been found."

Ward's fascination with odds and wagers was well-founded. Gambling had infested college football during this era. Big, traditional rivalries like Notre Dame-Army, Harvard-Yale attracted October, the Cincinnati Reds beat the Chicago White Sox five games to three in The 1919 World Series. To many observers, there was something wrong with the outcome of the baseball championship. Later, a grand jury discovered that many of the Chicago White White Sox players had taken cash payments from professional gamblers in order to "throw" the series.

According to Hunk Anderson, professional gamblers tried to get a "piece of the action" in the game with Army. "We were approached by gamblers before we left for the Army game, but that wasn't unusual. Every time we went away to play they tried to get us to place bets for them. But we always refused to get mixed up in that kind of business. And by we, I mean George also," Anderson said.

While Gipp didn't get involved with the gamblers or with betting for others, he was directly involved in the action during the Army game. On the night before the game Anderson went around and collected $2,100 from members of the Notre Dame team. Gipp contributed $400. Later that night Anderson met with the Army student manager, who told Anderson that the Army cadets would be able to cover that amount. The next morning, Anderson met the Cadet manager for breakfast. He had $2,100 and the two turned the money over to a German shoemaker. After putting the money in a safe, the shoemaker said, "Are you coming back?"

"...Don't worry, I'll be back," Anderson said.

In South Bend, normal activity came to a halt, as fans assembled at Cartier Field and at cigar stores and hotels to get the results and the play-by-play account of the game.

October 31, 1920

In his best game ever, Gipp led Notre Dame to a 27–17 come-from-behind victory.

Gipp was almost the entire Notre Dame offense, as he gained 150 yards on 20 carries and completed five of nine passes for 123 yards. It was perhaps the greatest one-man show in Notre Dame football history. After the game, newspapers from all over the country had lavish praise for Gipp.

After Notre Dame took the opening kickoff, it drove down the field where Chet Wynne fumbled. Cadet end Don Storck recovered the ball on the Army 37-yard line. Soon after this, Army back Walter French ran around left end for 40 yards, going past Gipp who made no attempt to tackle him. On the next play, with the ball on the Notre Dame 15-yard line, Army scored on a 15 yard off-tackle play by Lawrence. After French made the conversion, Notre Dame trailed 7–0.

On the ensuing kick-off Gipp brought the ball back to the 38-yard line before being gang-tackled by a horde of Cadets. On the next play, Gipp smashed off – tackle for eight yards. He then picked up the first down with a run up the middle. As the play ended, Hunk Anderson got in a fist fight with some player in the pile. Gipp came over to him. "What's the matter, Hunk?" Gipp asked.

"Some sonofabitch gave me the knee," Hunk said.

Gipp took off his helmet and took off after one of the Army players. The referee stepped in the middle and was able to restore order. But, he walked off 15 yards against Notre Dame for unsportsmanlike conduct. This put the Blue and Gold in a very bad position. It was now first down and 25 to go.

But Gipp responded to the pressure. On the next play, Gipp picked up the penalty yardage by sprinting around left end for 15 yards. Two plays later he broke into the clear and was prevented from scoring a touchdown by a saving tackle by French. After Brandy recovered his own fumble on a sneak up the middle, Gipp hit Roger Kiley with a long pass that brought the ball to the Cadet five-yard line. Johnny Mohardt plunged over for a touchdown and Gipp converted the point after to tie the score at 7.

Gipp was responsible for the second Notre Dame touchdown as he hit Kiley with a 40-yard bomb to give Notre Dame a 14–7 lead. But the lead didn't last long. After both teams were stopped, Notre Dame was forced to punt.

French picked up the ball on his own 40-yard line and cut through the Irish defense for a touchdown. From the sidelines Rockne was visibly upset with his team and Gipp in particular. Gipp had a chance to tackle French, but the Army back eluded him. It appeared that Gipp was uninterested in defense. As the teams lined up for the next kick-off Gipp told his teammates, "Don't worry, we'll get it back with more to spare." But, Notre Dame soon fell behind.

"Frequent penalties placed Notre Dame in a distressing position late in the second quarter. Disaster overtook Rockne, and then Gipp kicked out of bounds on his own ten-yard line. Three line plunges failed to gain the necessary distance for the cadets and French dropped back and kicked a field goal from the seven-yard line."

The first half was soon over and Notre Dame trailed, 17–14. Despite the offensive fireworks, it wasn't much of a half for Notre Dame. The penalties and the fumbles made Notre Dame look like a second rate football team. During the halftime break Rockne really ripped into his players.

"Rockne, giving one of his finest halftime orations to date, was really putting it to the boys for being three points behind," Anderson said. "He had just about finished when Gipp, standing nearby, asked for a drag on my cigarette. Rock looked up and caught George leaning against the door, his helmet rakishly set atop his head, blowing out smoke. Rock's face turned purple."

"What about you, Gipp?" he snapped, "I don't suppose you have any interest in this game?"

"Look, Rock," Gipp said, "I got $400 bet on this game, and I'm not about to blow it."

As the team walked out to the field, Gipp told his teammates, "Look, you guys give me a little help and I'll beat this Army team."

Notre Dame began the third quarter attempting the same trick play that worked against Nebraska earlier in the season. But, the Cadets had scouted Notre Dame and were able to stop the play.

Don Storck, an Army defender, said Gipp showed some humor even though he had been stopped. "On the preceding play Gipp had hit the middle of our line. As Notre Dame quickly lined up for the next play, George was slow in getting up, and the whole Notre Dame line relaxed, looking around at George. Ojay Larson, their center, was the only lineman to remain in position, bent over the ball. When quarterback Brandy called out to Gipp, 'Are you all right, George?' The ball was snapped to Mohardt. We were waiting for it and came rushing through the relaxed Notre Dame line, throwing Mohardt for a big loss with George under the pile. As George got up he said to me, 'Boy, we won't try that again — I could have been killed under there.' "

The third quarter was largely a defensive struggle and Army fought to keep its three point lead. Late in the quarter, Gipp began churning out some nice runs, and as the quarter ended Gipp ran the ball down to the Cadet 20-yard line. Gipp carried the ball up the middle for five yards on two carriers. From the 10-yard line, Brandy faked to Gipp and handed off to Mohardt who bolted into the end zone for a touchdown. After Gipp kicked the extra point Notre Dame led, 21–17.

After the ensuing kickoff, Army was held. Gipp passed the ball down the field again. He hit Roger Kiley with a 21 yarder and Frank Coughlin on a 26 yard tackle eligible play that gave Notre Dame the ball on the Cadet eight-yard line. While Army braced for another line plunge by Gipp, Brandy faked to him and Mohardt and gave the ball to Chet Wynne, who sneaked up the middle for the last touchdown of the day. The extra point gave Notre Dame a 28–17 lead.

The Cadets were stopped again. When Notre Dame got the ball back Gipp was given the ball one last time.

After plunging through the Army line for ten yards Rockne pulled him from the game.

"...I have never seen an athlete get the acclamation he (Gipp) received when he walked off the field that day. He was tired and pale and his face was a little bloody, and the crowd at West Point stood up and nobody applauded. It was thrilling — awed silence." said Roger Kiley.

Gipp spent the final three minutes of the Army game on the bench, cheering on his replacement. Father Charles L. O'Donnell said Gipp was active in cheering for Chet Wynne, who had trouble with fumbles earlier in the game.

"He had done everything that any football player had ever done upon a field, and he had done it better than most. Darkness was coming in on the bitter winds that swept across the plains as he sat there in his blanket, relaxed, pale, silent, crying a little, I think. Then suddenly he was on his feet. He leaped onto the bench; the blanket had fallen from his shoulders.

"Chet Wynne, our fullback, had made one of his amazing cuts through the line, good for some 15 or 20 yards. In a voice that could be heard, it seemed to me, above all the roar of the crowd, Gipp shouted: 'Yea, Chet!' as he stood there, self entirely forgotten, quivering from head to toe with joy and loyal pride in the achievement of a teammate."

Many had disputed Gipp's loyalty to Notre Dame. But, on this day no one could question it.

After the game, Army players had nothing but praise for Gipp. "Gipp just would not be stopped," said Donald Storck. "Whatever he did, it was with little effort but with grace and agility. His long-legged, elusive gallops through our defense on that day in late October were as difficult to stop as might be those of an antelope in an open field. His long strides made his deceptive speed difficult to time, with the result that most of the time we were tackling thin air."

The win for Notre Dame established Knute Rockne as an important figure in college football. For the Notre Dame football program it opened the door to national recognition. On November 3rd, Arch Ward wrote that Rockne had become a "miracle man".

"...Heralded as the 'miracle man' of American football, Head Coach Knute K. Rockne, of the Notre Dame football team, who has led the Gold and Blue to two successive victories over the Army, can have anything he wants around South Bend these days. Already the students of Notre Dame, alumni as well as undergraduates, hail him as the greatest coach in football.

"Last year Notre Dame was admitted to be one of the greatest teams in the country. It was the only undefeated team in the West. This season the pupils of Rockne are making even a greater name. It is improbable that anything can separate them from another western title."

"West Point worked every bit of strategy in the possession of a dozen or more coaches to defeat Notre Dame this year. It sent scouts to Nebraska and Valparaiso games. It augmented its staff the week before the game that every cadet might have an individual tutor. It worked Notre Dame plays against the varsity for days, but all to no avail, for Rockne's machine rose like a Goliath."

For George Gipp, the game against Army brought national recognition. New York sportswriters had heard about Gipp, but for many it was the only time they would ever see him play. After the game they compared him to other great backs of his era.

"George Gipp, the 'wonder man' of the west, is still the chief topic of conversation on Broadway. Not since the days of Ted Coy, of Yale, has an individual football player been showered with such praise as fell on Gipp in Sunday's New York papers. If Walter Camp overlooks Gipp when selecting his All-America team, things other than merit will enter into the makeup of the mythical aggregation."

"This man Gipp," states the *New York Herald,* "is All-American or there is no real All-American eleven this fall. If anything can be done on a football field that Gipp didn't do at West Point it isn't discernible to the naked eye. Notre Dame had two teams on the field — Gipp and ten other men. The Army couldn't stop Gipp no matter what they did. He was a Titan on attack and a concrete wall on defense."

After the game Hunk Anderson returned to the German shoemaker's shop and collected $4,000. Gipp's share was $800, and he and the rest of the Notre Dame team spent Saturday night in New York having a massive celebration. Early Sunday morning the Notre Dame football team boarded a train and headed back to South Bend. The train pulled into South Bend after midnight and was greeted by a large crowd. Gipp didn't like large celebrations, so he ducked out on the festivities.

The win against Army boosted interest in the game the following Saturday against Purdue. It was billed as a "homecoming" game, as many former Notre Dame players and alumni made plans to attend. Ticket sales were brisk. As for Gipp, the star back was feeling sore. He didn't practice until the Thursday before the game. On the day before the game, Rockne announced that Gipp would only see "limited" action in the Purdue game in order to save him for the game against Indiana the following week. For many observers, Purdue was a good team, but not nearly good enough to beat Notre Dame.

November 5, 1920

"...Bolstered by the presence of 'Red' Salmon and other stars of bygone days, Notre Dame will swing into the high powered section of western football tomorrow after noon at two o'clock. The opponent will be Purdue and the game will be played on Cartier Field before the largest gathering of fans that ever saw a football contest in northern Indiana."

"South Bend fans who want to take their last peep at George Gipp, the 'Babe Ruth of the Gridiron,' will do well to arrive at Cartier Field early. Coach Rockne announced that Gipp will play only the first few minutes of the game. Gipp is in poor shape for the battle and he is too valuable to use recklessly. After Rockne is satisfied that the fans have had a run for their money, the Tarzan of the football field will be yanked from the game and saved for the big struggles with Indiana and Northwestern in the future."

"The Purdue squad, 25 strong, reached the city early this afternoon, and is quartered at the Jefferson Hotel. The student delegation will arrive tomorrow. The Boilermakers, undaunted by the press agenting of the Gold and Blue clan, is oozing pepper like a lunch of Mexican tamales. Coach Scanlon is more than confident that his team has a fighting chance to win the game and he is going to see that his players extend themselves to the limit.

"The visiting team will be given a royal reception by the Notre Dame student body tonight. At 6:30 p.m. the boys will gather in the gymnasium for a short rehearsal after which a torch light parade, headed by the Studebaker Band, will march through the streets of South Bend to the Jefferson Hotel. Here the procession will stop and cheers for both teams will be yelled. Word from Newark, N.J. revealed that 'Red' Salmon, greatest football player in the history of Notre Dame, will be here for the game tomorrow. His great deeds of 1900 to 1904 on the gridiron enshrined his memory in the hearts of every devotee of the Blue and Gold forever.

"With Gipp out of the lineup during most of the game the team's attack will gravitate largely around Mohardt. If his performance at West Point and his work in scrimmage last night are criterions, he is more than capable of stepping into Gipp's position. Mohardt cracked the Cadets' line last week such as it had never been cracked before. When Gipp wasn't pounding off tackle or through the line, Mohardt was skirting the flanks.

His speed was dazzling and he hit the line much harder than Gipp. If his work were not overshadowed by the sensational performances of Gipp, Mohardt would loom as one of the greatest backfield men of the season in the eyes of the critics."

November 6, 1920

"...Over ten thousand fans are fighting for tickets for the Notre Dame-Purdue game on Cartier Field this afternoon. The advance sale was exhausted Friday noon and only general admission tickets, which must be procured at the gate, are available. Standing space will be at a premium when the two teams lineup at 2 p.m. this afternoon."

"An influx of Notre Dame alumni from all corners of the United States is one reason for the overflow crowd. The final appearance of Gipp, Coughlin, Smith, Brandy and Barry is another, and the strength of the opponent is the third. Local fans are convinced that the game will be a test down to bedrock for Notre Dame. Purdue has rallied splendidly since its early season setbacks at the hands of Chicago and Ohio State and Coach Scanlon, of the visiting aggregation, stated last night that his team" is ready for an upset.

"Purdue worked out behind closed gates for two hours on Cartier Field yesterday afternoon. The Boilermakers ought to be well acclimated by this time. Rockne is anticipating a smart overhead attack from the down state crew. It is improbable that Scanlon will attempt to batter down Notre Dame's concrete wall."

"The Notre Dame student body marched to the Oliver Hotel last night where they serenaded the Purdue party. After cheerleader Slaggart had strained his larynx with cheers for both teams, impromptu talks were given by Coach Scanlon, Captain Birk, Stanwood, Carmen, Wagner and Murphy of the visiting squad. Cries for 'Gipp, Gipp, All-American halfback,' were rendered in vain, for Gipp, as usual, was nowhere to be found at the time for speech making. Gipp limits his athletic activities to deeds on the gridiron."

Arch Ward also wrote that the win against Army fueled speculation that Notre Dame would play post-season games. "Reports from the east that negotiations have begun between Notre Dame and Harvard for a 1921 football game were denied by Rockne yesterday. He declared that no action has been taken on next year's schedule. He also put a quietus on the rumor that Notre Dame will meet Penn State in a post season game for the national championship."

"Georgetown is the only team that has approached us about a post season game," said Rockne, "and we refused the offer."

"There has been a persistent whisper in New York newspaper circles that a Notre Dame-Harvard game will supplant the Notre Dame-Army game as the big intersectional contest of the season next year. The Army, Gotham scribes contend, is no longer a real test for Notre Dame. The Gold and Blue has won five of the seven games played with the Cadets and another meeting would arouse little attention in the east."

"The Notre Dame faculty turned down an offer to play Harvard this fall, but whether it would frown on a

1921 contest, if such could be negotiated, has not been ascertained. Notre Dame's growing popularity in the east almost demands a contest with one of the so-called Big Three (Army, Harvard and Penn State)."

November 7, 1920

Gipp recovered, and his running and passing led Notre Dame to an easy 28–0 win over Purdue, before the largest crowd in the history of Cartier Field.

Gipp rushed for 129 yards on ten carries and completed 4 of 7 passes for 128 yards. The 257 yards of total offense was the second highest in his career, trailing only the 273 yards racked up against Army the week before.

Rockne started his second string line-up. "Second string men, most of whom were members of the 1919 freshmen eleven, faced Purdue in the opening grind. They played the visitors to a standstill for the first few minutes and then, after being forced to their own five-yard line, held the Boilermakers for a loss and took over the pigskin. The play worked back to the middle of the field before the quarter ended. Early in the second period 'Chet' Grant cut through the opposing defense, received a 30 yard pass from Castner and tore around the second defense of the Boilermakers for 40 yards and a touchdown."

"But Coach Scanlon's warriors seemed to realize they were being outplayed and swamped by a 'scrub' team so they went in and fought like young tigers. Inch by inch plunges coupled by Macklin's 12 yard run around right end, Wagner's nine yards around left and a forward pass which netted eight yards, gave the Purdue eleven its big chance to score in this period. They had the pigskin on the Notre Dame ten-yard line."

"Then something happened and the visitors' aspirations were shattered into bits—Rockne sent in his first team. Four additional attempts were all Purdue got before Notre Dame took over." A run by Wynne up the middle gained 15 yards and another by Barry gained nine. But, a penalty soon forced Notre Dame to punt. Gipp took the long snap from center and faked the punt.

Starting from his own 20-yard line Gipp ran through the Purdue line and shook off "tackle after tackle" before crossing the goal line and scoring a touchdown, that clinched the game for Notre Dame.

In the second half, Notre Dame added two more touchdowns to close out the scoring. After Notre Dame had a 28–0 lead, Gipp was pulled from the game to a standing ovation from the large crowd.

"Thousands of alumni sat in the bleachers and once more let their spirits rise to an unsurmountable height with pride—their old school had smeared the map with a grid record that would probably not be equaled in years. Every seat was taken and sidelines were crowded to the brim with spectators, who went wild with exuberant joy."

The win against Purdue showed that Notre Dame was not a one-man team. Rockne had achieved his season-long goal to mold a team that relied on all its players for its success. "While there is much credit being given each player on Rockne's eleven as an individual star, the biggest reason why the team wins is because these players work in harmony—they have been taught by

Rockne to play together and Saturday illustrated what a smooth running gridiron machine can do. Each man does his part. With such a machine it is impossible for any of America's football teams to better it when it is working up to par."

Cecil Cooley, a Boilermaker lineman, said Gipp was the main obstacle for Purdue. "Gipp was most evasive. He seemed to just step sideways at the right time or hop over me. Many times I was sure I had him, but most times ended up with empty hands. I can still remember very well looking around after he evaded me and see him going down the field weaving, sidestepping and twisting like a young colt that just got through an open gate."

After the victory over Purdue, Notre Dame prepared for its next game against interstate rival Indiana.

The games against Army and Purdue probably represented the high point of Gipp's career at Notre Dame. During the 1920 season and the fall semester Gipp had done several things to straighten himself out. His grades were up, and for the first time in his four years at Notre Dame, he was showing an active interest in academics. Rockne kept a close eye on Gipp, often sending a fellow player to follow Gipp. In late October, Gipp wrote a letter to a friend in Calumet and said that for the first time in years he was able to look forward.

The game against Indiana opened the door for speculation about the state championship in football. Since Notre Dame had beaten every other team on its schedule while Indiana had been undefeated since an opening day loss to Iowa, newspapers throughout the state hyped the contest.

"...A record breaking crowd will see the championship game. Washington Park, which has a seating capacity of 17,000, will be taxed to its capacity. Alumni organizations of both institutions have arranged for the entertainment of the two teams while in the capital city.

"Indiana has lost but one game this season. It got away on the wrong foot when it dropped the opening contest to Iowa, but since that time it has thumped everything in its path. Mississippi, Minnesota and Northwestern are among the Crimson's victims.

"Coach Rockne anticipates one of the hardest games of the season when he sends his charges against the Bloomington clan. From the standpoint of sterling competition it will rival the West Point game. (Indiana Coach) Stiehm has his men keyed up like a bunch of fiddlers. The whole Indiana squad saw Notre Dame beat Purdue and unless Rockne kept some of his best plays wrapped up the opponents will know pretty well where to exploit the attack.

"Notre Dame is in good physical trim for the test. If Rockne can keep his regular backfield — Brandy, Gipp, Mohardt and Wynne — intact during the week, Indianapolis fans are going to be treated to an exhibition of speed unprecedented in the history of Washington Park."

While many of the gamblers and football experts looked upon the Indiana game as an easy one for Notre Dame, Coach Rockne and the players saw the game as the ultimate test. Writing in *The South Bend Tribune* on November 11th, Arch Ward observed that many around South Bend were fearful of Indiana.

November 11, 1920

"...Contrary to past contests in which Notre Dame has entered this autumn no rock bound forecast of victory is audible on the university campus over the impending struggle with Indiana. Devotees of the Gold and Blue are convinced that Rockne's gridders are confronted with the supreme test of the season."

"Indiana is a team that is hard to dope. Stiehm's men invariably do the unexpected. Their most noteworthy example of this was in the game with Syracuse last season when they drubbed the easterners decisively in the biggest upset of the campaign. Circular letters emanating from Bloomington to alumni of the state institution carry the word that Notre Dame will be another Syracuse.

"Down state statisticians who are predicting a 30-point triumph for Notre Dame will awaken Sunday morning to find their forecasts bent and mangled, unless Rockne's athletes spring the biggest surprise of the year. Anyone who has seen a practice on Cartier Field this week will declare that the Notre Dame camp is preparing for the toughest contest of the season.

"Notre Dame is not anticipating defeat but it does look for a close score. Indiana has a powerful attack and a rugged defense. Press reports from Bloomington divulge the interesting bit of information that Notre Dame plays are executed by Crimson freshmen were easily solved by the varsity. It looks as though Stiehm's mission to Notre Dame last week on which occasion he was accompanied by his entire team was not in vain. Perhaps Stiehm has accomplished what scores of scouts have attempted in the past 32 years — a solution to Notre Dame's peculiar style of assault."

Gipp began to get recognition from eastern football writers during the week before the Indiana game. Walter Camp listed him among a list of star players and the *New York Herald* called Gipp the best back in the country.

On November 12th, word reached South Bend that Penn State had issued a challenge to the Notre Dame football team for a post-season game which would decide a national champion.

"A national football title may not be a myth this autumn. Not in many years have two teams stood out as prominently in their respective sections of the country as Penn State and Notre Dame. The Penn eleven is recognized as the peer of the east and Notre Dame has as good if not a better claim on the western title.

"Fred Wenck, a representative of the New York Baseball Club, reached the city this morning to confer with the Notre Dame athletic officials in regard to a post season game with Penn State for the national title. Mr. Wenck came from Philadelphia there he discussed the proposed game with Hugo Bezdek and other authorities of the Penn institution.

"Wenck proposes to bring the two teams to the Polo Grounds in New York on December 4th, the week following the Army-Navy Contest. A game between the sectional champions would draw a crowd of 40,000 people.

"Penn State is willing to tackle the Gold and Blue athletes, provided it defeats Pittsburgh and Lehigh in its remaining games. There is little doubt but that it will trounce both opponents, in event Penn State should fall down in either game, the New York promoter would match Notre Dame with Georgia Tech, the champion of the south."

A post-season game would have been very profitable for Notre Dame. It could have counted on thousands of dollars from its share of the gate receipts. Rockne was all for such a contest. The problem for him was the faculty, which had the authority to approve such contests. Final exams were approaching, and many instructors viewed another game as an unnecessary distraction for students. Here was another situation where profits and education conflicted.

On November 12th a squad of 40 Notre Dame players left South Bend via train and headed to Indianapolis. As the train pulled into Indianapolis, the entire city was buzzing in expectation of Saturday's game. *The South Bend Tribune* sent both Arch Ward and Eugene Kessler to the game.

Kessler reported that many gamblers were predicting a Notre Dame victory. "...Those feminine supporters who carried Crimson banners and wore the same colored arm bands into this city this morning seem to be more convinced as to the strength of their team than the stronger half of Indiana University. The men are hopeful of victory but not confident—they like their money better than their sympathy and confidence and bets were scarce throughout the day. Some Benders got three to one wagers, others got bets that Notre Dame will outpoint Indiana by 14 points and still other wagers were made that one of the Irish would outscore the entire Crimson eleven, but no even money was in sight."

The main focus of all the attention was Gipp. Kessler observed that stores all over Indianapolis had pictures of Gipp in their windows. "Wherever Gipp went he was followed by a host of admirers. Gipp started up Illinois Street and police thought it was the Indiana parade. He just can't evade the admirers."

Ward described the carnival like atmosphere in his article on game day.

November 13, 1920

"...Football fans from near and far are pouring into the capital city for the titular struggle between Notre Dame and Indiana. Hundreds of visitors are arriving on morning trains.

"Notre Dame was the first team to reach the city. The Indiana team arrives on a private car attached to the students' special just before noon today. The Bloomington rooters will hold a parade and their usual demonstration shortly after the noon hour.

"The largest crowd that ever attended a football game at Washington Park will see the contest. Ticket scalpers hold the only available seats. The advance sale points to a crowd of 17,000."

The game itself was one of the greatest in Notre Dame football history, as the Fighting Irish came back to defeat Indiana, 13–10, after being outplayed for most of the game. Gipp was held in check, gaining only 52 yards on 16 carries and getting 26 yards through the air on five pass attempts. He sustained a shoulder separation midway through the first half, but came into the game when Notre Dame needed a boost.

"...It was, perhaps, the greatest comeback ever recorded by a football team that Rockne's bunch pulled to save the day Saturday. The same backfield, which had been touted all season as world beaters were helpless throughout three long and draggy quarters and disappointed as fans who had never seen them perform at their natural stride. For the first three periods Indiana's beefy line withstood the on-rushes of all Rockne could send against them. The Gold and Blue defense was shattered into threads while Bell and Leonard crashed in from the wing positions and upset the mighty Gipp and powerful Mohardt before they got a good hold on the ball. In other words, Rockne's line looked about as good as a freshman squad."

Following the opening kick-off, Indiana drove down the field but was held on Notre Dame's 15-yard line. When Notre Dame took over it was unable to move the ball. Indiana was "up" for the game and Gipp was unable to gain much yardage. Late in the quarter, Gipp suffered the most serious injury of his career. After a rough tackle, Gipp got up slowly while holding his shoulder. "His shoulder was in such a crippled condition that it bothered him in running and making passes and his mouth and nose were bleeding from the unnecessary roughness on the part of his tacklers. So 'Rock' grasped the opportunity. He whispered something in the ear of Norm Barry and sent him in to replace Gipp."

Midway through the second quarter, Indiana drove down the field and kicked a field goal. After the Hoosiers took a 3–0 lead Notre Dame was unable to move. The half ended with Indiana holding the ball near mid-field. Fans were shocked to see Notre Dame trailing, but many assumed that once the second half got under way Notre Dame would be able to dominate. But, it was not to be. "Indiana, spurred on by its success in the first half, continued to 'play over their heads' and rushed the pigskin to the Notre Dame ten-yard line after taking the second half kickoff. From there the Hoosiers scored a touchdown on a pass play that fooled the Notre Dame defense."

The Indiana team was spurred on by the touchdown. It carried the ten-point lead into the fourth quarter and continued to dominate the game. It was the toughest defense Notre Dame had faced the entire season.

But, Notre Dame was able to fight back. With about ten minutes left in the game, Mohardt began moving the team. Following a good block by Barry, Mohardt ripped off a 25 yard gain that put the ball on the Indiana 20-yard line. Barry ripped off an 18 yard run around left end. This gave Notre Dame a first and goal.

Two line plunges failed to gain much yardage. After this, Gipp, with his shoulder heavily taped, trotted back onto the field. Gipp got the call and was stopped cold on third down.

On fourth down, Gipp got the call again. He gave it everything he had and smashed through the line for a touchdown. Gipp ran right in to the goal post and almost sent it tumbling to the ground. He converted the point after and Notre Dame trailed by three points.

The touchdown inspired Notre Dame. Following the kickoff the defense stopped Indiana. On third down 'Hunk' Anderson caused a fumble, which Notre Dame recovered. Gipp completed a pass which brought the ball down to the one-yard line. From there Joe Brandy sneaked over to give Notre Dame a 13–10 lead.

Notre Dame stopped Indiana on its next possession. Notre Dame was driving for a third touchdown when Brandy fumbled. With only five minutes left in the game Indiana began driving down field. It reached the Notre Dame 20-yard line before the defense stiffened. As time was running out, Indiana attempted a field goal. The kick was headed for the goal posts but faded and drifted off the right. After the missed field goal, Notre Dame was able to run out the clock.

The Indiana game was extremely bruising for many Notre Dame players. Several players were injured, none more seriously than Gipp. The Notre Dame team left Indianapolis on Sunday morning. Gipp rode the train back, but didn't leave when it arrived in South Bend. Instead, he continued on to Chicago, where he gave a clinic on drop-kicking to high school players at Loyola Academy, which was coached by Grover Malone, a former teammate of Gipp's. He spent three days in Chicago, trying to recover from a slight cold he got while teaching the drop-kick.

Back in South Bend, Gipp and other Notre Dame players were being praised for their effort against Indiana.

November 16, 1920

"...An unexplained display of grit that enabled Notre Dame to defeat Indiana Saturday was revealed yesterday when it became known that George Gipp played through the game with a fractured collar-bone.

"Gipp suffered the injury early in the first quarter of the contest. Though suffering excruciating pain, Gipp tried stubbornly to get away with long forward passes. He was forced to use a side arm motion instead of his usual overhand throw. Rockne, realizing that something was wrong with his star player, beckoned Gipp to the sidelines in the third quarter and substituted Barry.

"Gipp, however, insisted on playing out the game and he refused to heed his injury until he had started his mates toward victory by planting the ball behind the Indiana goal line early in the fourth quarter for Notre Dame's first touchdown."

"It is doubtful whether or not Gipp will be in shape to play in another game this season. The gritty halfback is anxious to get into the fray with Northwestern at Evanston Saturday as it will be his last big game in Gold and Blue togs, but Rockne said last night it is 'improbable' that Gipp will be used.

"Hunk Anderson is another athlete who performed throughout the Indiana game solely on his nerve. Anderson had a couple of ribs twisted into funny knots but he made no mention of this until Notre Dame has assured itself of a win."

Despite the heroic performances of Gipp and Anderson many observers thought Notre Dame had underestimated the Hoosiers. In his column, "Serving the Punch", *Tribune* sportswriter Eugene Kessler wrote that Notre Dame took the game for granted. "When Indiana stepped upon the field Saturday they looked beaten — but they were determined. Notre Dame boys were a little too confident — they thought they had the contest won before the whistle blew. Notre Dame players showed evidence of overwork—they went 'stale.' "

Arch Ward attributed the close game to overconfidence on the part of Notre Dame and rigorous scouting by Indiana. "Perhaps no team in modern football went to more trouble in preparing for a single opponent than Indiana did for Notre Dame. The clash with the South Bend men was the objective of the Crimson since Stiehm assembled his players last September. Notre Dame formations were rehearsed at Bloomington day in and day out."

"...This much is certain, however, in reviewing the game. Notre Dame carried little of the smart precision that characterized its work in past contests. The defense at times went sour. The linemen failed to tackle low and the backfield men didn't guard the opponents forward pass receivers in the manner which they are capable. In a word the team was on the bum."

In those days the Northwestern football team was quite formidable. During the 1920 season, the Wildcats had several impressive victories, including wins against several top rated opponents.

November 17, 1920

"...With visions of the western championship looming starkly through the mist beyond and handicapped by the absence of Gipp and Anderson, Notre Dame is making a desperate effort to rid itself of the jinx which threatens to mar the most glorious grid campaign in the history of the school."

"Rockne is taking every precaution to safeguard his men against possible injuries. Monday's and Tuesday's workouts were held indoors that the danger of slipping and sliding on a snow, covered field might be avoided."

"There will be hundreds of disappointed fans around Chicago Saturday night if they fail to see Gipp in action against Northwestern. Perhaps Gipp has no more admirers anywhere in the country than in Chicago."

On Wednesday, Gipp arrived back in South Bend. He confined himself to Sorin Hall, trying to rest his shoulder and do something for a slight cold.

On November 18th, the Notre Dame faculty decided to reject a post-season contest with Penn State. While the game had been actively considered prior to the Indiana game, the injuries to Gipp and Anderson and final exams weighed heavily. At the time it didn't look like Gipp would be able to play another game, so Rockne decided against a game with Penn State.

Coach Rockne decided to give his players a rest on Wednesday before the Northwestern game. He visited Gipp several hours before the train was scheduled to leave South Bend.

"Think you're up for the trip?" Rockne asked.

"I suppose so," George replied.

"If you're not feeling up to par when we get there, I don't intend on using you," Rockne said.

"That's jake with me."

Gipp's injury and pronouncements by Rockne did not dim the enthusiasm for the game. Notre Dame's allotment of 4,000 tickets was gone by Thursday morning. Temporary bleachers were erected as demand for tickets reached unprecedented levels. Many Notre Dame alumni had settled in Chicago. The Alumni Association had designated November 20th as George Gipp Day.

By Friday, Gipp was feeling well enough to travel. At 6:45 p.m. the South Shore train pulled out of South Bend taking Gipp and 29 other players. Because Gipp was on the train, rumors spread that he was going to start the Northwestern game.

"...Persistent rumors that Gipp will start against the Purple were denied by Rockne last night. Gipp, who returned from Chicago, where he underwent treatment for his injured shoulder, is anxious to get into the fray, but Rockne contends that it would be foolhardy to expose Gipp's injured shoulder to another jolt that might mean permanent disability."

Gipp was not included in the starting lineup. As the team checked into the Auditorium Hotel on Friday night, it was uncertain whether Gipp would see any action.

On Saturday, nearly 30 train cars, filled with Notre Dame rooters arrived in Evanston. Every ticket was sold and by the time the game started only "standing room" remained.

As the players lined up for the opening kickoff, many of the fans groaned because Gipp was not in the lineup. Through the first half fans booed nearly every move made by Rockne. The chant of "We Want Gipp. We Want Gipp" filled the air.

After a scoreless first quarter, Notre Dame scored its first touchdown in the second quarter following a fumbled punt. A pass from Brandy to Anderson gave Notre Dame a 7–0 lead. Notre Dame scored again right before halftime, as a long drive culminated in a touchdown.

Early in the third quarter Northwestern scored on a 50 yard run. This made the score 14–7. But, it was as close as the Wildcats would get. When Northwestern got the ball again, Coughlin intercepted a pass on the Wildcats 35-yard line. A long run by Barry gave Notre Dame the ball on the one-yard line where Notre Dame was able to push the ball over on a short pass from Mohardt to E. Anderson. As the third quarter ended, Notre Dame was in complete control of the game, leading 21–7.

As the fourth quarter began the chanting for Gipp became louder. Finally, with about 12 minutes left in the game Gipp was inserted in the lineup. On his first play, Gipp hit Eddie Anderson with a perfect pass that Anderson ran in for a touchdown. The 35 yard pass play gave Notre Dame a 27–7 lead. After the Notre Dame defense stopped Northwestern, it took over near midfield. This time Gipp tried a running play but he coughed up the ball. It was clear that his high fever caused limited mobility for Gipp.

With a couple of minutes left in the game, Gipp got another chance. He hit Anderson with another pass, and the speedy end ran 50 yards for a touchdown.

Throughout sports history there has been a controversy over just who was the receiver on the long pass play. *The South Bend Tribune,* which had a correspondent at the game credits the reception to Anderson. But, for many years the touchdown was credited to Norman Barry. Notre Dame record books listed a 70 yard pass from Gipp to Barry as a record for years. This is one of the controversies that marked early football.

Record-keeping was often not accurate and it is quite likely that no true account will ever be known.

But nothing can detract from Gipp's performance. He completed five of six passes in the fourth quarter for 129 yards. Barry later said Gipp would have broken every passing record if he had used the smaller, modern football. "With the smaller ball that's in use now, I feel sure George would have broken every pass record to date. He used to say, 'You be there, and the ball will be there.' "

With about one minute left in the game, Gipp fielded a Northwestern punt. By this time the players on Northwestern's team knew Gipp was in a weakened condition and they gently guided him down. The game ended with Notre Dame a 33–7 victor. Several Northwestern players had high praise for Gipp.

Graham Penfield, the captain of Northwestern's team said the long pass to Anderson was "one of the best passes I've ever seen thrown."

"When we came out for the second half, there was George warming up on the sidelines and throwing passes at least 50 yards," Penfield said. "He went into the game later and, in spite of his illness, proved himself a very fine player and with such good blocking that I don't remember whether or not I ever got near enough to even try to tackle him."

After the game Gipp's throat was extremely sore. Rockne said that he probably should have kept him off the field. The ice covered field "with a wind off Lake Michigan that was cutting us all to the bone" could not have been good for someone who had a cold and a sore throat.

It was clear that Gipp would not be in any condition to play against the Michigan Aggies on Thanksgiving day. The last time Gipp missed a game, Notre Dame lost, and many thought the season would be ruined if he wouldn't be able to play.

November 22, 1920
"...Notre Dame will seek its 18th consecutive football victory when it meets the Michigan Aggies at East Lansing, Thursday, in the season's final. Not since Rockne last led his men into the Michigan capital, in 1918, have they tasted defeat.

"It was the loss of Gipp that marred an otherwise perfect season for Notre Dame in the turbulent year of 1918. After plowing through one of the hardest schedules ever handed a Gold and Blue eleven without a defeat, the jinx stepped in and plugged Gipp and Bahan, the team's stars, from the lineup on the eve of the Michigan Aggie game and the locals were defeated, 13-7.

"Similar conditions prevail this autumn. Notre Dame has met with remarkable success and measured by comparative scores, the South Bend eleven carries a wide margin over the Aggies. Gipp, who was injured in the Indiana game a week ago, may be out of the struggle, however, and his absence may bring about another 1918 disaster."

On Monday night, Gipp and the rest of the Notre Dame team were honored at a dinner thrown by South Bend businessmen. During the speach-making, Gipp told 'Hunk' Anderson he probably wouldn't be able to play against the Aggies.

"Hunk, I feel terrible," Gipp said. "My throat's cutting me up, and I got a high fever."

"You better talk it over with Rock and maybe go to the hospital." Hunk said.

After meeting with the coach, Gipp decided to enter St. Joseph Hospital. When he was admitted he complained about a sore throat and the chills.

While Gipp was in the hospital the rest of the Notre Dame team got ready for the Michigan Aggies. On November 23rd, Arch Ward previewed the game, and reported that Gipp could possibly play.

November 23, 1920

"...Fans throughout this part of the country are watching the impending struggle between Notre Dame and the Michigan Aggies at East Lansing Thursday with undiminished interest, despite Notre Dame's wide margin of superiority.

"Notre Dame will face the Wolverines without the services of Chet Wynne, the hard-hitting fullback who covered himself with glory at Evanston Saturday. Wynne established his name firmly in western football by his great work against Northwestern.

"With the exception of Wynne, the Notre Dame squad is in good condition and is prepared to battle to maintain its prestige. George Gipp, who favored some 20,000 gridiron followers with a 15 minute performance at Evanston Saturday, will play against the Aggies should the going get too rough for his mates."

November 24, 1920

While Gipp remained at St. Joseph's with a 104 degree temperature, speculation was rampant that a post season game would be scheduled against either Princeton, Ohio State or Oregon. Ohio State was very interested in a game. Promoters received approval from Coach Rockne and began making plans for a contest at Comiskey Park after the season was over. Ohio State's contract with the Big Ten conference required that it get permission from every other school in the conference before it could play a game against Notre Dame or any other school. Its season still had one week to go, and so the promoters decided to wait and see how the Buckeyes fared in their last game.

Notre Dame had its last practice of the season on November 24th. Ward wrote that the last game would end the career of most of Notre Dame's backfield. "The backfield, however, will suffer most from this year's graduations. Gipp, Brandy and Barry are a trio of backs whose worth is attested by the extent of their fame. These men have been the nucleus of Notre Dame's smashing attack for three seasons and it will be some years to come before a western eleven boasts of such an aggregation of star performers."

"The team will leave for Lansing a wide favorite over the Aggies, despite the fact that Pottsy Clark's men have piled up scores approaching the century mark on some of Michigan's college teams. The Aggies record with teams of caliber doesn't warrant a prediction of victory over Notre Dame."

As Notre Dame's football team boarded the train for East Lansing, Gipp remained behind in the hospital. A doctor was brought in to examine Gipp on the day of the game. His illness was diagnosed as tonsillitis. The hospital reported his condition as serious, but issued a statement that Gipp would be out of the hospital in a short period of time.

The game against the Aggies was decided very quickly. Notre Dame started the game with its second stringers, and the subs responded. On the opening kick-off, Gipp's replacement, D. Coughlin, returned the kick 80 yards for a touchdown.

After the opening score the contest settled down. Notre Dame's defense was firmly in control. The half ended with the Aggies holding the ball on their two-yard line. A series of passes opened things up in the third quarter and Notre Dame scored two more touchdowns. In the fourth quarter, Hunk Anderson blocked a punt and this led to the final score. The 25–0 victory over the Aggies gave Notre Dame its second straight undefeated season.

The Death of the Gipper

Gipp's condition began improving two or three days after he was admitted to the hospital. His fever was reduced to around 100 degrees. But, the persistent sore throat wouldn't go away. The doctors tried a mixture of honey and glycerine in an attempt to provide relief.

Earlier in the year, before football season, Gipp's personal doctor in Laurium had suggested that Gipp have his tonsils removed. But Gipp rejected the idea and continued to suffer through frequent sore throats. On November 29th his condition got worse. "George Gipp, idol of football fans, is in serious condition at St. Joseph's Hospital. His ailment which was formerly reported as tonsillitis has developed into pneumonia, according to information given out at the hospital this morning. Coaches Knute Rockne and Walter Halas called upon Gipp yesterday afternoon. Mr. Rockne says he expects the Notre Dame star to be over the danger mark in two or three days."

As Gipp's condition worsened, prospects for a post season game diminished. Newspapers around the country began printing daily bulletins on Gipp's condition.

November 30, 1920

"...The University of Notre Dame campus where devotees of the Gold and Blue congregate to discuss past gridiron triumphs was quiet last night. George Gipp, around whom football gossip gravitates is lying critically ill at St. Joseph's Hospital with a severe attack of pneumonia and plans for post season games have been temporarily delayed.

"Gipp's condition was pronounced grave by the attending physician last night. A decided change for the better or worse is anticipated before another night has passed. Gipp's relatives have been notified of his condition and his mother reached the city yesterday. No visitors are permitted to see the football monarch.

"Pneumonia was the culmination of an illness that started as tonsillitis the forepart of last week. Gipp was taken to the hospital the latter part of the week, but his condition was not considered serious until yesterday.

"Negotiations for a game in the far west will depend largely on the condition of Gipp."

On the morning of the 30th, *The Tribune* reported that Gipp's condition was "slightly improved".

During the time of his illness, Gipp received more acclaim than he ever had when he was well. He was named captain of the all-Western team on November 30th. The next day he received a great boost.

December 1, 1920

"...George Gipp, far famed Notre Dame athlete, may browse in Chicago baseball pastures next summer if negotiations which have been opened for his services by the Cubs are successful. President Bill Veeck Sr. of the Chicago National League Club made Gipp a lucrative offer yesterday, but the Gold and Blue star is not worrying over future athletic activities just now. He is summoning all his strength to deal a body blow to a disease that has made a vicious attempt to deprive him of further achievements.

"Gipp's condition was unchanged this morning. He was improved yesterday morning, but suffered a relapse in the afternoon and his attending physician stated he was still in a critical condition. Hopes of his recovery are brighter, however, than 24 hours ago and if he pulls through the day without further setbacks, he will have passed the crisis.

"Gipp, of course, was too ill yesterday to give consideration to the proposal from the Cubs. Johnny Evers, manager of the Cubs, admires Gipp's ability as a baseball as well as a football player and the Trojan is sure Gipp will qualify as a regular outfielder after a few weeks of training.

"Gipp's fame on the gridiron would make him a valuable asset to the box office of any ball team in the country. The turnstiles at the North Side park will click more rapidly than ever if Gipp" plays for the Cubs next season."

His medical condition, while it had improved somewhat still remained bad. Specialists were called in from Chicago. On December 1st, Dr. T. O'Connor, an eye, ear, nose and throat specialist arrived from Chicago. He was followed by another noted physician, Dr. C.H. Johnson. The two remained at Gipp's side for nearly 24 hours without a break.

For his high fever, Gipp was given Dover's powder. He also drank several shots of whiskey and cold compresses were applied to his head. His fever finally subsided around noon on December 2nd. For the next day or two, Gipp regained some of his strength. He was able to hold a normal conversation with members of his family and with Coach Rockne and other members of the football team.

Late in November, the celebrated sportswriter Walter Camp, named Gipp to his All-America team. The selections were announced in *Collier's Weekly.* "...In the backfield Gipp of Notre Dame gets the first place on account of his versatility and power, able as he is to punt, drop kick, forward pass, run, tackle – in fact do anything that any backfield man could ever be required to do and do it in well-nigh superlative fashion. He drop-kicked on his freshman team 62 yards. When a man who has been taken off with a badly injured shoulder can go in on a pinch and carry the ball over the goal line to get his team an absolutely necessary touchdown, something of the man's power can well be understood."

The news of Gipp's selection on the Walter Camp All-America team reached South Bend just as Gipp was starting to have a slight recovery. When Rockne found out about his selection, he decided to visit Gipp and see if the news would cheer him up.

"How does that make you feel?" Rockne asked, "knowing you're the first player in Notre Dame's history to receive the honor."

"Well, that's jake, Rock," Gipp said.

By this time, Hunk Anderson was visiting Gipp on a daily basis. He later said Gipp was in high spirits for most of the first few days at the hospital.

On December 3rd, all hope for a post season contest vanished as a proposed contest with Oregon fell through. Arch Ward wrote that Gipp's illness had dampened the enthusiasm for another game. Originally, the Oregon game was to be set for New Years Day. But, Coach Rockne thought his team wouldn't be ready for a game until Gipp's fate was determined. For this reason, offers of post season contest were rejected. Meanwhile, Coach Rockne went about the business of setting up a schedule for the 1921 season.

December 3, 1920

"...Offers for 1921 contests are pouring into Coach Rockne's official chamber and within a week or two the schedule will take form. Heading the list of applicants for next season's games is Georgia Tech. The southern champions want Notre Dame to journey to Atlanta for the game. A Notre Dame-Tech game would do much to clear up national football attention."

On December 4th, Rockne attended a coaches meeting in Chicago and was able to set up football games with Indiana, Iowa and Purdue for the 1921 season. On December 6th, Rockne concluded negotiations with Army and was able to set up a game with the Cadets.

As for Gipp's condition, *The South Bend Tribune* reported little progress on December 6th. "Gipp has made little improvement the past two days and fear is expressed that his condition may take a downward trend at any moment."

At this time Rockne began to experience some regret over Gipp's condition. In a special article by Edward Thierry, Rockne said he was upset that Gipp was able to convince him to allow him to play against Northwestern.

"...Being a star athlete has its penalties. George Gipp, Notre Dame's brilliant halfback and hailed as the season's greatest college football player, pushed himself into the hero class, and when he was badly injured he had to live up to his heroic role or disappoint the crowds.

"He begged to be allowed to go back into a game against Indiana, although his shoulder was dislocated. The crowd thought he was cast iron. A week later he begged again to get into the game against Northwestern. Chicago crowds were yelling for the Notre Dame hero.

"Gipp felt he had to go in and play, no matter how it tortured him.

"Three days after the Northwestern game, Gipp had a tickling in his throat. It was tonsillitis. Then came pneumonia. Gloom hung over Notre Dame's 2,000 students as bulletins from the sickroom were anxiously read. He is still in a critical condition.

ß'Some people thought Gipp's life was in jeopardy because of his bulldog determination' to play in spite of his injured shoulder. As a matter of fact, physicians said there wasn't any connection between his illness and football.

"Nevertheless, Knute Rockne, the football coach, is sorry he weakened under Gipp's pleadings and let him play when he was not in first class condition."

"Our men have to be physically fit or they can't play," said Rockne, "for the primary aim of college athletics is and always should be, to benefit the boys physically. All the gridiron fame in the world isn't worth ruining a single boy's health."

But Rockne's sentiments notwithstanding, it is clear a central aim of college athletics has always been fund raising. This aim, combined with alumni loyalty and campus enthusiasm has motivated many football players. Also, gambling has played no small role in this interest, where the aim of college football changed from being a recreational activity for young men on college campuses, to a profit-making endeavor. Basically, little has changed at Notre Dame, or at many other major colleges which emphasize football and basketball. What has changed the sport from a fun activity to a serious business was the prospects of larger gate rvenues and an increased media interest in the sport. Football offered colleges and universities a financial lifeline, and many were eager to jump at it.

Gipp was at the forefront of this change. He was a "professional" who excelled at his craft. It didn't really matter that he didn't care much for the books. His role at Notre Dame was important in the change from athletic pastime to a sports business.

Gipp's brother Matthew, who arrived in South Bend on the 6th, told Thierry that he didn't think Gipp's troubles were caused by football.

"Those tonsils have been bothering him for years," said Matthew Gipp, "The doctor says George would have been 80 percent better if he'd had those tonsils out before he played." By the 8th of December, Gipp had been receiving so many visitors, the hospital had to put a guard at the door. Students from the campus offered to help Gipp out by donating blood.

December 8, 1920

"...One hundred fifty students of Notre Dame university yesterday volunteered to give their blood in the effort to save the life of George Gipp, the star halfback who lies critically ill. When Gipp's condition took a turn for the worse late Monday, the physicians believed that blood transfusion would be necessary, and when this was learned the students volunteered. However, after ten had been selected to undergo tests, Gipp rallied and his condition was so much improved this morning that it was decided not to make the transfusion."

His recovery continued, and by December 10th, *The South Bend Tribune* reported his condition improved:

December 10, 1920

"...George Gipp, Notre Dame star football player, this morning had regained the strength lost yesterday. His condition was improved and he once more showed signs of recovery. Yesterday it appeared as though Gipp was yielding slowly to the disease which has held him fast to his bed for the past three weeks.

"The proposed Notre Dame-Pacific Fleet game at San Francisco Christmas Day has been cancelled. The game was conditionally accepted last week pending Gipp's recovery. Notre Dame athletes have no desire to enter another contest this season with their compatriot standing on the doormat of death. They are disappointed, to be sure, that their visions of a great trip have been shattered, but no wail arises from the Gold and Blue camp."

"Gipp is suffering from streptoccic throat trouble and the toxins are affecting his whole system. He is delirious much of the time. His mother, brother and sister have clung steadfastly by his side since he became dangerously ill ten days ago."

After visits by family and friends, Gipp began to show an interest in the Catholic religion. Gipp had never been too interested in religion until this time, an many viewed his interest in religion as a way that Gipp realized the seriousness of his disease.

By the evening of December 12th, Gipp's condition took a turn for the worse. His temperature shot up again, and this time doctors could see little reason for optimism. While he improved slightly on the morning of December 13th, by mid-day the hospital called Gipp's family and urged them to come by his bedside.

So, Gipp's mother, sister and brother came to the hospital. When they arrived in his room, Gipp was almost delirious. Coach Rockne soon entered the room and stood behind the Gipps. Gipp cried out, "I'm not going to die—I'm going to play one more game for Rock."

The nurse asked some other visitors to leave and Gipp began whispering to Rockne.

"I've got to go, Rock. It's all right, I'm not afraid, sometime, Rock, when the team's up against it, when things are going wrong and the breaks are beating the boys—tell them to go in there with all they've got and win one for the Gipper. I don't know where I'll be then, Rock, but I'll know about it, and I'll be happy."

"Shortly after noon on Tuesday, December 14th, Gipp looked up from his bed, smiled at his mother, and then lapsed into a coma. Early on the morning of the 15th, Gipp finally succumbed.

Letters, wires and telegrams poured into Notre Dame from all over the country after Gipp died. They came from governors, congressmen, alumni and players who lined up against Gipp when he played. The praise for Gipp came from nearly the entire midwest.

"George Gipp was the greatest halfback who has ever represented Notre Dame, and his unquestionable ability was surpassed by a grit which featured all his work on the gridiron and was the marvel of his attending physicians. The outstanding feature of his character was a deep affection for his mother, and in his death I feel a keen personal loss," said Knute Rockne in a statement for the press.

Gipp's body was taken to the McGann Funeral Parlor, which was located at 333 N. Michigan Street. Classes at Notre Dame were suspended on December 17th to allow students to pay their last respects. A requiem mass was held at Sacred Heart Church early in the morning. After the mass, a long procession took the casket to the train station. A reporter from *The South Bend Tribune*, probably Arch Ward, wrote about the final moments.

"...When the first of the escort reached the station, the lines separated and the students bared their heads to the snow as the body of their Gipper went on to its appointed end. Here, where Notre Dame could do no more for its wonder man, the procession waited. As the Chicago train arrived the crowd moved forward towards the casket, which was being prepared to enter the baggage car. A blanket of flowers on which the Notre Dame monogram was mounted, the last symbol of the love of the Notre Dame student body, remained atop it, destined to accompany the the body to its final resting place."

"Telephone poles, baggage trucks, and every point of vantage at the station were utilized as the casket was elevated to the door of the car. As though by an unspoken command a hat came off here and there, and in a flash the crowd was bareheaded. Silently, with almost defiant faces, the students gazed at the departing form of their idol."

The train pulled into Chicago around 1:00 p.m. A large crowd gathered, many of them wanting to see Gipp one more time. The train was in for a four-hour lay-over and some asked railroad officials to put the body on display. This request was turned down.

Gipp finally came back to Calumet. On Saturday afternoon, December 18th, his funeral was held at The Light Guard Armory. Nearly the whole town attended. Several of Gipp's teammates came along. Frank Coughlin was asked to prepare the eulogy.

"George Gipp was perhaps the greatest athlete I have ever known. He was a man among men, brilliant and unassuming, and has endeared himself to the heart of every Notre Dame student by his athletic prowess, magnetic personality, keen mind, and his great love for the old school. He will forever be remembered as a friend, a student, an athlete, and a gentleman, for to know him was to love him."

Other players also had glowing praise for Gipp. "George was without doubt one of the greatest players of all time. The way he could punt, drop kick, and run the ball was more than brilliant. He could run from any point on the field, combining speed and power with a hip twist that made him the most dangerous man I ever saw in action," said Hunk Anderson. "His play was a technical treat for football connoisseurs of that time — and how he could drift through interference. His magnetic leadership, his genius as an open field runner, his spine-tingling dashes and his matchless morale endeared him to thousands and made football history. But although a great football hero, he was not the type of athlete who expected everything to be handed him on a golden platter just because he was a star. Gipp was a man, and what he he got he earned."

In the years that passed after his death, Notre Dame continued to dominate football in the midwest. Rockne soon established the Four Horsemen, and this innovation helped Notre Dame stack up more victories.

EPILOGUE

By 1928, Notre Dame had been able to dominate. But the 1928 football season started out badly. Two early loses left Notre Dame a decided underdog as it prepared to face Army.

But, Rockne was able to rev up his players. They came from behind to defeat Army, 12–6. Legend has it that Rockne told his players to "Win one for the Gipper" in a halftime speech. But, this scenario is highly unlikely. Notre Dame was not trailing in the game at half-time. The score was 0–0, and so Rockne was not in a desperate situation. The team was already playing inspired football, and at this point there was probably little Rockne could say to further inspire his team.

In the third quarter, Notre Dame fell behind 6–0. It came back with a touchdown late in the third quarter to tie the score at 6. In the fourth quarter, a long pass on 3rd and 30 from Niemiec to O'Brien gave Notre Dame the win.

The legend has always maintained that it was Chevigny who crashed through the line and said "That's one for the Gipper," as he tied the game and as he scored the winning touchdown. But, Chevigny was injured during the third quarter and had little to do with Notre Dame scoring its touchdowns. So, if he did not score the touchdowns, he could not have said "That's one for the Gipper." The legend of George Gipp, like most popularized life stories, favors his accomplishments. He was a balanced person with weaknesses, as well as great athletic talents. Certainly the movie, *Knute Rockne-All American* is an idealized portrayal of Gipp. He was not the angelic "All-American" that actor Ronald Reagan portrayed. The movie shows Rockne as being rather intolerant of gamblers and their influence on college football. It has a scene where Rockne rousts gamblers from the Notre Dame locker-room. It is doubtful, judging from accounts of Hunk Anderson and others, that this ever really occurred. Rockne had to know about the gambling that members of the Notre Dame team engaged in. He also had to know about Gipp's penchant for shooting pool, playing cards and staying out late. These activities were absent in the film. The "Gipper" that Ronald Reagan portrayed was a Hollywood image of a real American sports hero.

About the Author

George Gekas

George Gekas has always been an avid sports participant in all sports from high school on through his Army career. This book is the result of a lifetime of association with people who were directly in touch with George Gipp during his illustrious career, from his beginnings in Calumet, Michigan, where James Gekas, the author's father owned a restaurant, through his historic football feats at Notre Dame.

George Gipp's closest friend, Angelo Stappas, was known to George Gekas as "Uncle Angie" and used to work at the restaurant. During the years between 1903 and 1918 George Gipp was a regular.

Uncle Angie strongly influenced George Gekas during his youth and gave him his first introduction to gambling. Like George Gipp, Angie's gambling philosophy was a common one, namely, to never excel at a sport until the stakes were high. George Gekas later used this philosophy during his years in the Army, when he won big pots while bowling.

Angie used to tell him stories of how he and Gipp loved the life of a gambler. These stories, at heart, inspired George Gekas with many anecdotes, to write *The Life and Times of George Gipp,* the true life story of the "Gipper", Notre Dame's most popular football athlete.

After the war, George returned to Calumet and operated his father's restaurant. Then in 1948, Angie and George moved to Arizona where they bought into The Varsity Restaurant, an established and popular attraction for players and coaches of the University of Arizona football team. There, George was considered the unofficial recruiter, fondly referred to as the "Coach."

The Arizona restaurant featured a back room with pool tables, dice boards and plenty of poker. During the winter months, George recalls top notch gamblers from the era of George Gipp, like Nick "The Greek" and "Titanic Thomas" often coming by. Sometime these gamblers would get bored with standard games like poker and they would invent other, more interesting games.

They would bet on almost anything. For example, Angie would make bets on who could flip coins onto the cross-beams of the restaurant ceiling. On other days they looked for outdoor games. One favorite was a unique version of golf; not the game played by the pro's, but rather it used a pool stick, with which they would stroke a cue ball down the golf course. It took more than an hour and between nearly 100 strokes, but the high stakes made this golf far more interesting than any other event in Arizona.

In 1958, George Gekas sold his interest in the Varsity Restaurant and returned to the Midwest. During the 1960s and 1970s, he was the General Manager of the Chicago Press Club, a favorite hang-out for local sports personalities and news reporters.

A visitor to the Club was Pat O'Brien, the popular movie star who played the part of Knute Rockne in the movie, *Knute Rockne-All American*. He and George had many long rap sessions regarding the Gipper. Pat O'Brien once remarked to George, "You know more about George Gipp than I do. I wish you could meet Ronald Reagan out in Hollywood and bend his ear a little."

One day in 1965, when George was in Las Vegas, Angie gave him more encouragement: "I hope you remembered all the stories I told you about Gipp. I hope someday you can let the world know about the real Gipp, I'm really surprised that Notre Dame has never put up a statue to recognize the Gipper."

Among other writings, George Gekas has also written *Hospitality Career*, a correspondence course in restaurant and club management. George Gekas today resides in Chicago with his wife Helen.

Acknowledgements

The author expresses his gratitude and appreciation to Victor Crown, reporter for Chicago radio station WBEZ-FM, who has worked with several regional radio stations and is the author of many newspaper articles for Chicagoland neighborhood newspapers. His ability to research history has aided this as well as many other investigative consulting projects, most notably in the areas of politics and government. Victor Crown holds a Master's degree from Northwestern University Medill School of Journalism and lives in Chicago.

Gratitude and acknowledgements are also extended to the David Coltman, George Pappas, Edward "Moose" Krause, Joe Mishica, Dr. William M. Scholl of the College of Podiatric Medicine Library; The Parkside Restaurant; Jethrow Kyles and George Sirenko; The Memorial Library of Notre Dame; Eddie Gold and Chuck Gekas of the *Chicago Sun Times.*

Bibliography and Sources

Books:

Anderson, Hunk, and Emil Klosinski. *Notre Dame, Chicago Bears and "Hunk".*

Beach, James. *The Story of a Proud Heritage*, Notre Dame Football. GV/958/N6/B4.

Chelland, Patrick. *One for the Gipper* GV/939/G53/C47.

Condon, David, Chet Grant and Robert Best. *Notre Dame Football Golden.* GV/958/V54/C66/1982.

Gildea, William. *The Fighting Irish.* GV/958/N6/G54.

Lovelace, Delos W. *Rockne of Notre Dame* GV/939/R6/L6.

Murdoch, Angus. *Boom Cooper.*

Stuhldrier, Harry A. *Knute Rockne Manbuilder.*

Weyland, Alexander A. *Football Immortals.* GV/939/41/W4.

Newspapers:

The South Bend Tribune, South Bend Times, Houghton Mining Gazette, Los Angeles Times, and *The New York Times.*

Index